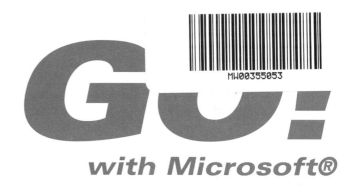

GO!

with Microsoft®

Internet Explorer 11

Getting Started

GO!

with Microsoft®

Internet Explorer 11
Getting Started

Shelley Gaskin and
Heddy Pritchard

Boston   Columbus   Indianapolis   New York   San Francisco   Upper Saddle River
Amsterdam   Cape Town   Dubai   London   Madrid   Milan   Munich   Paris   Montréal   Toronto
Delhi   Mexico City   São Paulo   Sydney   Hong Kong   Seoul   Singapore   Taipei   Tokyo

Vice President, Career Skills: Andrew Gilfillan
Senior Editor: Jenifer Niles
Team Lead, Project Management: Laura Burgess
Project Manager: Rhonda Aversa
Program Manager: Emily Biberger
Development Editor: Ginny Munroe
Editorial Assistant: Melissa Davis
Director of Product Marketing: Maggie Waples
Director of Field Marketing: Leigh Ann Sims
Field Marketing Managers: Brad Forrester & Joanna Sabella
Marketing Coordinator: Susan Osterlitz
Senior Operations Specialist: Maura Zaldivar

Senior Art Director: Diane Ernsberger
Interior and Cover Design: Diane Ernsberger
Cover Photo: © photobar/Fotolia
Associate Director of Design: Blair Brown
Digital Media Editor: Eric Hakanson
Director of Media Development: Taylor Ragan
Media Project Manager, Production: John Cassar
Full-Service Project Management: PreMediaGlobal
Composition: PreMediaGlobal
Printer/Binder: RR Donnelley
Cover Printer: Lehigh-Phoenix Color
Text Font: MinionPro

Credits and acknowledgments borrowed from other sources and reproduced, with permission, in this textbook appear on the appropriate page within text. Microsoft and/or its respective suppliers make no representations about the suitability of the information contained in the documents and related graphics published as part of the services for any purpose. All such documents and related graphics are provided "as is" without warranty of any kind.

Microsoft and/or its respective suppliers hereby disclaim all warranties and conditions with regard to this information, including all warranties and conditions of merchantability, whether express, implied or statutory, fitness for a particular purpose, title and non-infringement. In no event shall Microsoft and/or its respective suppliers be liable for any special, indirect or consequential damages or any damages whatsoever resulting from loss of use, data or profits, whether in an action of contract, negligence or other tortious action, arising out of or in connection with the use or performance of information available from the services.

The documents and related graphics contained herein could include technical inaccuracies or typographical errors. Changes are periodically added to the information herein. Microsoft and/or its respective suppliers may make improvements and/or changes in the product(s) and/or the program(s) described herein at any time.

Microsoft® and Windows® are registered trademarks of the Microsoft Corporation in the U.S.A. and other countries. This book is not sponsored or endorsed by or affiliated with the Microsoft Corporation.

Library of Congress Control Number: 2014939474

10 9 8 7 6 5 4 3 2 1

PEARSON

ISBN 10: 0-13-384763-2
ISBN 13: 978-0-13-384763-5

Table of Contents

About the Authors

Shelley Gaskin, Series Editor, is a professor in the Business and Computer Technology Division at Pasadena City College in Pasadena, California. She holds a bachelor's degree in Business Administration from Robert Morris College (Pennsylvania), a master's degree in Business from Northern Illinois University, and a doctorate in Adult and Community Education from Ball State University (Indiana). Before joining Pasadena City College, she spent 12 years in the computer industry, where she was a systems analyst, sales representative, and director of Customer Education with Unisys Corporation. She also worked for Ernst & Young on the development of large systems applications for their clients. She has written and developed training materials for custom systems applications in both the public and private sector and has also written and edited numerous computer application textbooks.

This book is dedicated to my students, who inspire me every day.

Heddy Pritchard is an adjunct professor in the School of Engineering and Technology (EnTec) at Miami Dade College and in the School of Office Careers/Computer Science/Computer Science-Industrial at Broward College. She holds a bachelor's degree in Computer Information Systems from Florida Atlantic University and a master's degree in Computer Information Systems from Nova Southeastern University (Florida). She has been a programmer/analyst for 26+ years and involved in the development of numerous applications.

This book is dedicated to students who want to improve
their lives with the use of computers.

GO! with Internet Explorer 11

GO! with Internet Explorer 11 is the right solution for you and your students in today's fast-moving, mobile environment. The GO! Series content focuses on the real-world job skills students need to succeed in the workforce. They learn to use Internet Explorer 11 by working step-by-step through practical job-related projects that put the core functionality of Internet Explorer 11 in context. And as has always been true of the GO! Series, students learn the important concepts when they need them, and they never get lost in instruction, because the GO! Series uses Microsoft procedural syntax. Students learn how and learn why—at the teachable moment.

What's New

New Design reflects the look of Windows 8 and Office 2013 and enhances readability.

Enhanced Chapter Opener now includes a deeper introduction to the A & B instructional projects and more highly defined chapter Objectives and Learning Outcomes.

New GO! Learn It Online Section at the end of the chapter indicates where various student learning activities can be found, including multiple choice and matching activities.

New Styles for In-Text Boxed Content: Another Way, Notes, More Knowledge, Alerts, and **new *By Touch* instructions** are included in line with the instruction and not in the margins so that the student is more likely to read this information.

New Visual Summary focuses on the four key concepts to remember from each chapter.

New Review and Assessment Guide summarizes the end-of-chapter assessments for a quick overview of the different types and levels of assignments and assessments for each chapter.

New End-of-Chapter Key Term Glossary with Definitions for each chapter.

Teach the Course You Want in Less Time

A Microsoft® Office textbook designed for student success!

- **Project-Based** – Students learn by creating projects that they will use in the real world.

- **Microsoft Procedural Syntax** – Steps are written to put students in the right place at the right time.

- **Teachable Moment** – Expository text is woven into the steps—at the moment students need to know it—not chunked together in a block of text that will go unread.

- **Sequential Pagination** – Students have actual page numbers instead of confusing letters and abbreviations.

Student Outcomes and Learning Objectives – Objectives are clustered around projects that result in student outcomes.

Design – Provides a more visually appealing and concise display of important content.

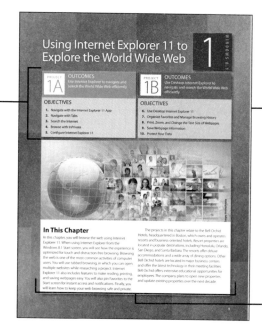

Scenario – Each chapter opens with a job-related scenario that sets the stage for the projects the student will create.

Project Activities – A project summary stated clearly and quickly.

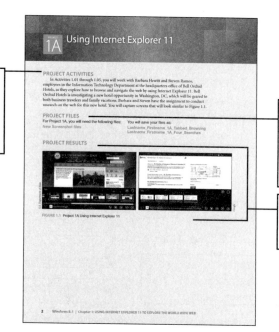

Project Files – Clearly show students which files are needed for the project and the names they will use to save their documents.

Project Results – Show students what successful completion looks like.

In-Text Features

Another Way, Notes, *More* Knowledge, Alerts, and By Touch Instructions

Microsoft Procedural Syntax –
Steps are written to put the student at the right place at the right time.

Color Coding – Each chapter has two instructional projects, which is less overwhelming for students than one large chapter project. The two projects are differentiated by different colored numbering and headings.

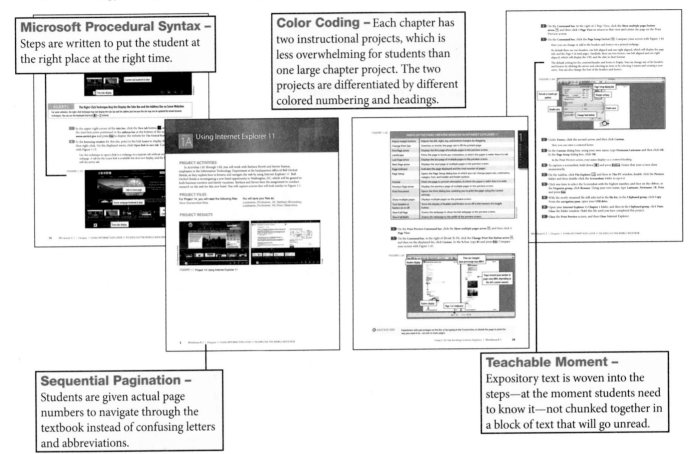

Sequential Pagination –
Students are given actual page numbers to navigate through the textbook instead of confusing letters and abbreviations.

Teachable Moment –
Expository text is woven into the steps—at the moment students need to know it—not chunked together in a block of text that will go unread.

End-of-Chapter

Content-Based Assessments – Assessments with defined solutions.

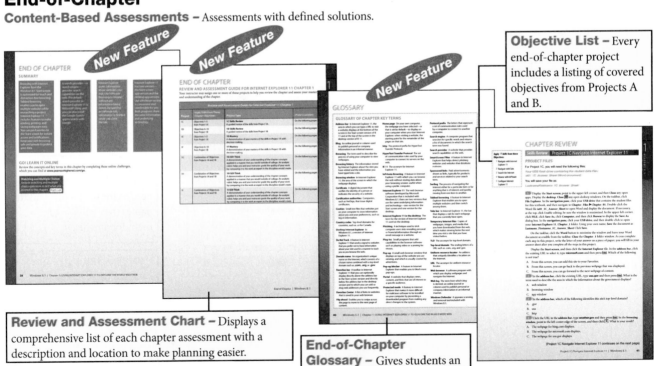

Objective List – Every end-of-chapter project includes a listing of covered objectives from Projects A and B.

Review and Assessment Chart – Displays a comprehensive list of each chapter assessment with a description and location to make planning easier.

End-of-Chapter Glossary – Gives students an easy way to review key terms.

End-of-Chapter

Content-Based Assessments – Assessments with defined solutions. (continued)

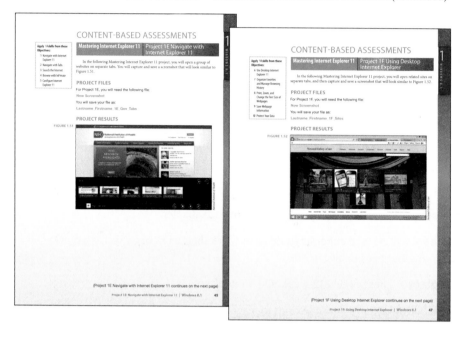

End-of-Chapter

Outcomes-Based Assessments – Assessments with open-ended solutions.

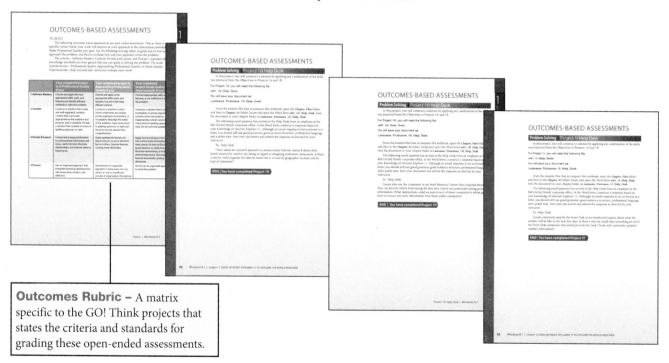

Outcomes Rubric – A matrix specific to the GO! Think projects that states the criteria and standards for grading these open-ended assessments.

Student Materials

Student Data Files – All student data files are available to all on the Companion Website: www.pearsonhighered.com/go.

Instructor Materials

All Instructor and Student materials available at pearsonhighered .com/go

Student Assignment Tracker – Lists all the assignments for the chapter. Just add the course information, due dates, and points. Providing these to students ensures they will know what is due and when.

Scripted Lectures – A script to guide your classroom lecture of each instructional project.

Annotated Solution Files – Coupled with the scorecards, these create a grading and scoring system that makes grading easy and efficient.

PowerPoint Lectures – PowerPoint presentations for each chapter.

Scoring Rubrics – Can be used either by students to check their work or by you as a quick check-off for the items that need to be corrected.

Syllabus Templates – For 8-week, 12-week, and 16-week courses.

Test Bank – Includes a variety of test questions for each chapter.

Companion Website – Online content such as the Online Chapter Review, Glossary, and Student Data Files are all at www.pearsonhighered.com/go.

Reviewers

GO! Focus Group Participants

Kenneth Mayer	Heald College
Carolyn Borne	Louisiana State University
Toribio Matamoros	Miami Dade College
Lynn Keane	University of South Carolina
Terri Hayes	Broward College
Michelle Carter	Paradise Valley Community College

GO! Reviewers

Abul Sheikh	Abraham Baldwin Agricultural College
John Percy	Atlantic Cape Community College
Janette Hicks	Binghamton University
Shannon Ogden	Black River Technical College
Karen May	Blinn College
Susan Fry	Boise State University
Chigurupati Rani	Borough of Manhattan Community College / CUNY
Ellen Glazer	Broward College
Kate LeGrand	Broward College
Mike Puopolo	Bunker Hill Community College
Nicole Lytle-Kosola	California State University, San Bernardino
Nisheeth Agrawal	Calhoun Community College
Pedro Diaz-Gomez	Cameron
Linda Friedel	Central Arizona College
Gregg Smith	Central Community College
Norm Cregger	Central Michigan University
Lisa LaCaria	Central Piedmont Community College
Steve Siedschlag	Chaffey College
Terri Helfand	Chaffey College
Susan Mills	Chambersburg
Mandy Reininger	Chemeketa Community College
Connie Crossley	Cincinnati State Technical and Community College
Marjorie Deutsch	City University of New York - Queensborough Community College
Mary Ann Zlotow	College of DuPage
Christine Bohnsak	College of Lake County
Gertrude Brier	College of Staten Island
Sharon Brown	College of The Albemarle
Terry Rigsby	Columbia College
Vicki Brooks	Columbia College
Donald Hames	Delgado Community College
Kristen King	Eastern Kentucky University
Kathie Richer	Edmonds Community College
Gary Smith	Elmhurst College
Wendi Kappersw	Embry-Riddle Aeronautical University
Nancy Woolridge	Fullerton College
Abigail Miller	Gateway Community & Technical College
Deep Ramanayake	Gateway Community & Technical College
Gwen White	Gateway Community & Technical College
Debbie Glinert	Gloria K School
Dana Smith	Golf Academy of America
Mary Locke	Greenville Technical College
Diane Marie Roselli	Harrisburg Area Community College
Linda Arnold	Harrisburg Area Community College - Lebanon
Daniel Schoedel	Harrisburg Area Community College - York Campus
Ken Mayer	Heald College
Xiaodong Qiao	Heald College
Donna Lamprecht	Hopkinsville Community College
Kristen Lancaster	Hopkinsville Community College
Johnny Hurley	Iowa Lakes Community College
Linda Halverson	Iowa Lakes Community College
Sarah Kilgo	Isothermal Community College
Chris DeGeare	Jefferson College
David McNair	Jefferson College
Diane Santurri	Johnson & Wales University
Roland Sparks	Johnson & Wales University
Ram Raghuraman	Joliet Junior College
Eduardo Suniga	Lansing Community College
Kenneth A. Hyatt	Lone Star College - Kingwood
Glenn Gray	Lone Star College - North Harris
Gene Carbonaro	Long Beach City College
Betty Pearman	Los Medanos College
Diane Kosharek	Madison College
Peter Meggison	Massasoit Community College
George Gabb	Miami Dade College
Lennie Alice Cooper	Miami Dade College
Richard Mabjish	Miami Dade College
Victor Giol	Miami Dade College
John Meir	Midlands Technical College
Greg Pauley	Moberly Area Community College
Catherine Glod	Mohawk Valley Community College
Robert Huyck	Mohawk Valley Community College
Kevin Engellant	Montana Western
Philip Lee	Nashville State Community College
Ruth Neal	Navarro College
Sharron Jordan	Navarro College
Richard Dale	New Mexico State University
Lori Townsend	Niagara County Community College
Judson Curry	North Park University
Mary Zegarski	Northampton Community College
Neal Stenlund	Northern Virginia Community College
Michael Goeken	Northwest Vista College
Mary Beth Tarver	Northwestern State University
Amy Rutledge	Oakland University
Marcia Braddock	Okefenokee Technical College
Richard Stocke	Oklahoma State University - OKC
Jane Stam	Onondaga Community College
Mike Michaelson	Palomar College
Kungwen (Dave) Chu	Purdue University Calumet
Wendy Ford	City University of New York - Queensborough Community College
Lewis Hall	Riverside City College
Karen Acree	San Juan College
Tim Ellis	Schoolcraft College
Dan Combellick	Scottsdale Community College
Pat Serrano	Scottsdale Community College
Rose Hendrickson	Sheridan College
Kit Carson	South Georgia College
Rebecca Futch	South Georgia State College
Brad Hagy	Southern Illinois University Carbondale
Mimi Spain	Southern Maine Community College
David Parker	Southern Oregon University
Madeline Baugher	Southwestern Oklahoma State University
Brian Holbert	St. Johns River State College
Bunny Howard	St. Johns River State College
Stephanie Cook	State College of Florida
Sharon Wavle	Tompkins Cortland Community College
George Fiori	Tri-County Technical College
Steve St. John	Tulsa Community College
Karen Thessing	University of Central Arkansas
Richard McMahon	University of Houston - Downtown
Shohreh Hashemi	University of Houston - Downtown
Donna Petty	Wallace Community College
Julia Bell	Walters State Community College
Ruby Kowaney	West Los Angeles College
Casey Thompson	Wiregrass Georgia Technical College
DeAnnia Clements	Wiregrass Georgia Technical College

Using Internet Explorer 11 to Explore the World Wide Web

1

1A
OUTCOMES
Use Internet Explorer to navigate and search the World Wide Web efficiently

PROJECT
1B
OUTCOMES
Use Desktop Internet Explorer to navigate and search the World Wide Web efficiently

OBJECTIVES

1. Navigate with the Internet Explorer 11 App
2. Navigate with Tabs
3. Search the Internet
4. Browse with InPrivate
5. Configure Internet Explorer 11

OBJECTIVES

6. Use Desktop Internet Explorer 11
7. Organize Favorites and Manage Browsing History
8. Print, Zoom, and Change the Text Size of Webpages
9. Save Webpage Information
10. Protect Your Data

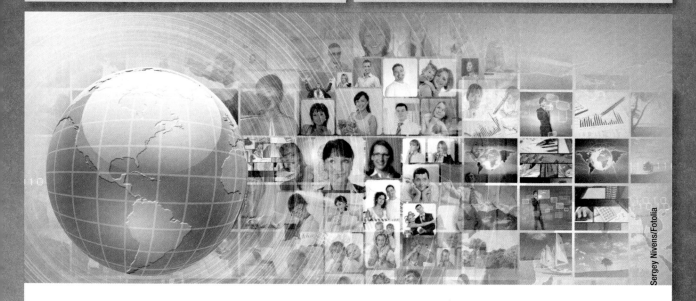

Sergey Nivens/Fotolia

In This Chapter

In this chapter, you will browse the web using Internet Explorer 11. When using Internet Explorer from the Windows 8.1 Start screen, you will see how the experience is optimized for touch and distraction-free browsing. Browsing the web is one of the most common activities of computer users. You will use tabbed browsing, in which you can open multiple websites while researching a project. Internet Explorer 11 also includes features to make reading, printing, and saving webpages easy. You will also pin Favorites to the Start screen for instant access and notifications. Finally, you will learn how to keep your web browsing safe and private.

The projects in this chapter relate to the Bell Orchid Hotels, headquartered in Boston, which owns and operates resorts and business-oriented hotels. Resort properties are located in popular destinations, including Honolulu, Orlando, San Diego, and Santa Barbara. The resorts offer deluxe accommodations and a wide array of dining options. Other Bell Orchid hotels are located in major business centers and offer the latest technology in their meeting facilities. Bell Orchid offers extensive educational opportunities for employees. The company plans to open new properties and update existing properties over the next decade.

Using Internet Explorer 11

PROJECT ACTIVITIES

In Activities 1.01 through 1.05, you will work with Barbara Hewitt and Steven Ramos, employees in the Information Technology Department at the headquarters office of Bell Orchid Hotels, as they explore how to browse and navigate the web by using Internet Explorer 11. Bell Orchid Hotels is investigating a new hotel opportunity in Washington, DC, which will be geared to both business travelers and family vacations. Barbara and Steven have the assignment to conduct research on the web for this new hotel. You will capture screens that will look similar to Figure 1.1.

PROJECT FILES

For Project 1A, you will need the following files:

New Screenshot files

You will save your files as:

Lastname_Firstname_1A_Tabbed_Browsing
Lastname_Firstname_1A_Four_Searches

PROJECT RESULTS

FIGURE 1.1 Project 1A Using Internet Explorer 11

> **NOTE**   If You Are Using a Touchscreen
>
> - Tap an item to click it.
> - Press and hold for a few seconds to right-click; release when the information or command displays.
> - Touch the screen with two or more fingers, and then pinch together to zoom in or stretch your fingers apart to zoom out.
> - Slide your finger on the screen to scroll—slide left to scroll right and slide right to scroll left.
> - Slide to rearrange—similar to dragging with a mouse.
> - Swipe from edge—from right to display charms; from left to expose open apps, snap apps, or close apps; from top or bottom to show commands or close an app.
> - Swipe to select—slide an item a short distance with a quick movement to select that item and bring up commands, if any.

Objective 1   Navigate with the Internet Explorer 11 App

A **web browser** is a software program that you use to display webpages and navigate the Internet. **Internet Explorer 11**—also referred to as **IE 11**—is the web browser software developed by Microsoft Corporation and that is included with Windows 8.1.

When launched from the Windows 8.1 Start screen by clicking the Internet Explorer tile, the browser displays in the full-screen, immersive view like other Windows 8.1 apps—no distracting windows, toolbars, or menus display. IE 11 is built with a touchscreen interface but works equally well with a keyboard and mouse.

Browsing is the term used to describe the process of using your computer to view webpages. **Surfing** refers to the process of navigating the Internet either for a particular item or for anything that is of interest, and then quickly moving from one item to another.

Browsing the web is one of the most common activities performed by individuals who use computers. Common tasks that you perform on the Internet might include looking at your favorite news sites, managing your finances with your bank, conducting research, shopping, sending email messages, using social media sites such as Facebook or Twitter, or reading or writing entries in a **blog**. A blog—short for **web log**—is an online journal or column used to publish personal or company information in an informal manner. For example, the developers of Microsoft Word maintain a blog of information about using Word at **http://blogs.office.com/b/microsoft-word/**.

> **NOTE**   This Book Assumes You Are Using a Mouse and Keyboard but You Can Also Use Touch
>
> The instruction in this textbook uses terminology that assumes you are using a mouse and keyboard, but you need only substitute the gestures listed earlier to move through the instruction easily using touch. If a touch gesture needs more clarification, a *By Touch* box will assist you in using the correct gesture. Because more precision is needed for many desktop operations, touching with a stylus pen may be preferable to touch using your fingers. When working with Windows Store apps, finger gestures are precise.

Activity 1.01   Navigating with Internet Explorer 11

1 ▶ Display your **Start screen**, and then compare your screen with Figure 1.2.

> If you have been using Windows 8.1 on your computer, your Start screen will differ. For purposes of this instruction, just be sure you can see the Internet Explorer tile.

FIGURE 1.2

2 On the **Start screen**, click the **Internet Explorer** tile, and notice the **address bar** at the bottom of the screen.

The **address bar** displays at the bottom of the screen where you can type the address of the website you want to visit or type a term for which you want to search. Buttons for various tools display on the right. The website that displays will vary, depending on whether you have set a home page or if you have visited a webpage and then closed Internet Explorer 11. The default site is Microsoft's MSN site—yours may differ.

Because Internet Explorer 11 is optimized for a touchscreen experience, the address bar displays at the bottom of the screen where it is easy to use and reach when using touch gestures.

The address bar displays when you open a webpage. When the address bar is not displayed, it will reappear when you right-click or swipe up from the bottom of the screen.

3 Point to the bottom of the screen, click the existing web address—the URL—to select it, type **bing.com** and then click or tap **Go** ⊙ or press Enter. Compare your screen with Figure 1.3, and then take a moment to study the table in Figure 1.4.

URL is the acronym for **uniform resource locator**, which is an address that uniquely identifies a location on the Internet.

On most webpages, you can click links to other webpages. For example, the Bing site displays links to trending information and other news items.

FIGURE 1.3

Browsing window

Photo image will differ from this one shown

Forward button

Page tools/App available button

Tabs bar

URL typed in address bar

Favorites

Site icon

Tabs

Back button

Refresh button

FIGURE 1.4

PARTS OF THE INTERNET EXPLORER SCREEN	
Screen Part	**Description**
Address bar	Provides the area in which you type the URL for the site you want to visit and which also works as a search box; also provides buttons for tools and navigation.
Address box	Provides an area to type a web address or a search term.
Back button	Displays the previous page you visited; activates after you visit more than one webpage.
Browsing window	Displays the webpage content for the site you are visiting.
Favorites button	Displays the favorites bar with a tile for each webpage based on the favorites selection. On the upper-left corner of the favorites bar, click the favorites arrow to view all your favorite sites or a subset of your favorite sites. On the upper-right corner of the favorites bar, the Add to favorites, Pin site, and Share buttons display. Use the Add to favorites button to add the current webpage to your favorite sites. Use the Pin site button to pin the current webpage to the Start screen. Use the Share button to share the current webpage by sending an email or posting to a social network.
Forward button	Displays the next page if you used the Back button.
Page tools/App available button	Displays a menu to *Get app for this site* if the site has an app available, to search on the current webpage, to report website problems to Microsoft, to view the same page in the Internet Explorer desktop application, to view a list of files recently downloaded from the web, or to change browser options. A + on the button indicates that the displayed site has an app available, which you can install from the menu.
Refresh button	Reloads the webpage you are viewing to see updates since the last time you viewed it.
Site icon	Displays the icon of the website currently displayed in the browsing window; the Internet Explorer icon displays if IE 11 detects no icon for the site.
Tabs bar	Displays touch-friendly tabs for each webpage currently open and buttons to open a new tab and display tab tools.
Tabs button	Displays the tabs bar with a touch-friendly tab for each webpage currently open. On the upper-right corner of the tabs bar, the New tab and Tab tools buttons display. Use the New tab button to open a website in a new tab. Use the Tab tools button to manage tabs.

4 In the **address bar**, click to select the existing URL, and then compare your screen with Figure 1.5.

> When you click the existing URL in the address bar, Internet Explorer 11 may display websites that you visit frequently.

FIGURE 1.5

Pinned (may or may not display; yours will differ)

URL selected in address bar

5 With the current URL selected, type **www.usa.gov** and press Enter. Compare your screen with Figure 1.6.

> The website for the U.S. government displays. By typing in the address bar and pressing Enter, the new URL opens.

> As you type in the address bar, Internet Explorer 11 will use its autocomplete feature to assist you in reaching sites that you visited previously, are Pinned or Favorites, or are popular URLs. The tiles for these sites may also display, and you can click or tap the tile to access the website. Or, as soon as the complete URL is visible, you can press Enter or click or tap the **Go** button ⊙.

> Because of the Windows 8.1 roaming feature, you will be able to access recent webpages on all your PCs.

FIGURE 1.6

Icon for usa.gov site displays in address bar

A URL contains the *protocol prefix*—in this instance, *http*—which stands for *HyperText Transfer Protocol*. HTTP represents the set of communication rules used by your computer to connect to servers on the web. Internet Explorer defaults to the *http* prefix, so it is not necessary to type it, even though it is part of the URL for this site.

The protocol prefix is followed by a colon and the separators //.

A URL also contains the *domain name*—in this instance, *www.usa.gov*. A domain name is an organization's unique name on the Internet and consists of a chosen name combined with a *top-level domain* such as *.com*, *.org*, or *.gov*. *TLD* is the acronym for top-level domain.

ALERT! **Websites Update Content Frequently**

As you progress through the projects in this chapter, the pictures and text of various websites may not match your screens exactly because website administrators frequently update content. This will not affect your ability to complete the projects successfully.

---

6 Take a moment to study the table in Figure 1.7 to become familiar with top-level domains.

> There are two types of top-level domains—the generic top-level domains, such as .com, .org, and .gov, and the *country codes*, such as .ca for Canada, .cn for China, and .uk for United Kingdom.

FIGURE 1.7

COMMON DOMAIN NAME EXTENSIONS AND ORGANIZATION TYPES	
Domain Name Extension	**Organization Type**
.com	Commercial businesses and companies.
.net	Formerly for Internet service providers and other communications-oriented organizations, but now open to anyone to register.
.org	Usually nonprofit organizations, but open to anyone to register.
.edu	U.S. educational only.
.gov	U.S. government only.
.info	An open domain; anyone can register.
.mobi	Mobile devices.
.name	Individuals and families.
.biz	Usually small businesses.

Shelley Gaskin

7 ▶ Point to the bottom of the screen, click the URL text to select it, type **weather.gov** and then press [Enter] to display the website for the **National Weather Service**.

8 ▶ In the **address bar**, on the left, click **Back** one time.

The Back button takes you to the previous page you visited and is active after you visit more than one webpage.

9 ▶ In the **address bar**, on the right, click **Forward** ▣ to move to the next page—the **National Weather Service** website.

Recall that the Forward button takes you to the next page if you used the Back button.

10 ▶ In the **address bar**, click the URL text to select it, type **abcnews.com** and then press [Enter]. On the **Page tools/App available** button ⊘, notice that a + displays on the button. Click **Page tools/App available** ⊘ to display a menu, and then compare your screen with Figure 1.8.

A + on the Page tools/App available button indicates that this site has an app available, which you can install by clicking the button and then on the menu, choosing *Get app for this site*.

An app is useful for sites that you want to explore and navigate without using a browser. Especially on a touch device, apps enable you to enjoy the experience without using a lot of navigation buttons.

FIGURE 1.8

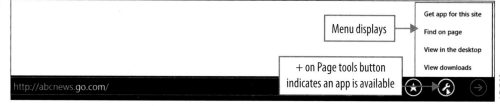

ABC News

More Knowledge **Using Flip Ahead**

On a touchscreen device, the *flip ahead* feature enables you to swipe across the page to move to the next page of content. This is especially useful in news sites that support flip ahead: for example, the Windows 8.1 News and Finance apps. Flip ahead is usually enabled by default. To check your system to be sure this feature is enabled, from the browsing window, display the charms, click the Settings charm, click Privacy, and then notice the setting under *Flip ahead with page prediction*.

11 ▶ Click the **Back** button ◉ one time to return to the website for the National Weather Service, and then on the **address bar**, click **Favorites** ◉. On the displayed Favorites bar, click **Pin site** ◉, and then compare your screen with Figure 1.9.

> The logo and name for the National Weather Service display, along with Previous and Next buttons on the sides for personalizing your Start screen tile.

FIGURE 1.9

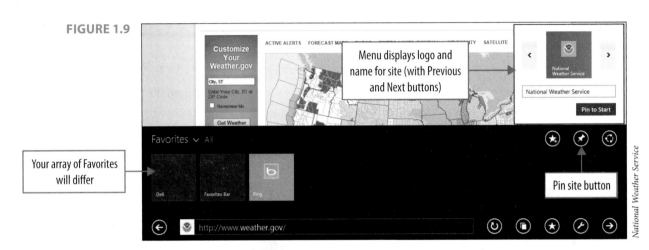

12 ▶ Click **Pin to Start** to pin this site to your Start screen.

13 ▶ In the **address bar**, click the URL text to select it, and then type **office.microsoft.com** and press Enter.

14 ▶ Move your pointer up about half way on the screen and away from the **address bar**, and then point to the left edge of the screen to display the **Back** button ◀ in the **browsing window**. Compare your screen with Figure 1.10.

> The area of the screen that displays the contents of the website is the ***browsing window***. When you point to the left edge of the screen, a Back button ◀ displays. You can click the button, or by touch, use a flick gesture to go back to the previous page.

FIGURE 1.10

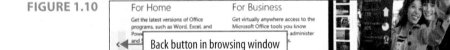

15 ▶ If necessary, point to the left edge of the screen again to display the **Back** button ◀, and then click the button to go back to the National Weather Service website.

↻ **BY TOUCH**   Flick the **Back** button ◀ to the right.

---

16 ▶ Point to the center-right side of the **browsing window**, click the **Forward** button ▶ one time to display the next page—the **Microsoft Office** page.

↻ **BY TOUCH**   Flick the **Forward** button ▶ to the left.

---

17 ▸ Point to the top of the screen to display a title bar, and then in the upper right corner, click the [×] to close Internet Explorer 11 and return to the desktop (the default setting in Windows 8.1 Update) or redisplay the Start screen.

> **More Knowledge** | **Dismiss and Redisplay the Address Bar**
>
> To hide the address bar, click anywhere on a displayed webpage. To redisplay the address bar with your frequently viewed sites, press [Alt] + [D] or [Ctrl] + [L].

Objective 2 Navigate with Tabs

Tabbed browsing is a feature in Internet Explorer that enables you to open multiple websites and then switch among them. In this activity, you will work with Barbara and Steven, who are conducting research on the new hotel in Washington, DC.

Activity 1.02 | Navigating with Tabs

1 ▸ From your **Start screen**, click the **Internet Explorer** tile.

The displayed website will be your home page if one is set or the last webpage you displayed before closing Internet Explorer.

2 ▸ Click in the **address bar** to select the existing URL, type **microsoft.com** and then press [Enter].

3 ▸ If necessary, point to an empty area of the **browsing window** until the [⇱] pointer displays, and then right-click to display the **tabs bar** and the **address bar**. Compare your screen with Figure 1.11.

Use this right-click technique anytime you want to redisplay the address bar and the tabs bar.

The *tabs bar*, located just above the address bar, displays a tab for each webpage that you currently have open—only one tab displays because only one webpage is open. The address bar displays at the bottom of the screen.

Unless you open a website in a new tab, each site you open replaces the previous site that was open. At the right side of the tabs bar, the New tab and Tab tools buttons display. Use the New tab button to open a website in a new tab. Use the Tab tools button to manage tabs.

FIGURE 1.11

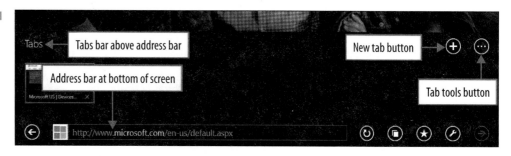

↻ **ANOTHER WAY**   Press [⊞] + [Z] to display the tabs bar and the address bar.

↻ **BY TOUCH**   Swipe down a short distance from the top of the screen to display the tabs bar and the address bar.

---

4 ▸ On the right side of the **tabs bar**, click the **New tab** button [⊕], and notice that the insertion point displays at the bottom of the screen ready for you to type a new URL or search term.

Side margin: 1 WINDOWS 8.1

5 Type **www.whitehouse.gov** and press [Enter] to display the official website for **The White House**.

As you type, recall that Internet Explorer 11 will use autocomplete to suggest sites you have visited, favorite or pinned sites, or sites that IE 11 recognizes as a popular site.

6 Point to an empty area of the **browsing window** to display the [⬉] pointer, hold down [⊞] and press [Z]. Compare your screen with Figure 1.12.

The tabs bar displays tabs for the previous webpage you had open—the Microsoft site—and the current site, which is bordered in blue.

FIGURE 1.12

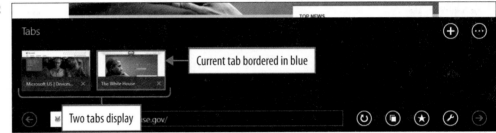

Whitehouse

ALERT!   **The Right-Click Technique May Not Display the Tabs Bar and the Address Bar on Some Websites**

For some websites, the right-click technique may not display the tabs bar and the address bar because the site may not be updated for newer browser techniques. You can use the keyboard shortcut [⊞] + [Z] instead.

---

7 In the upper-right corner of the **tabs bar**, click the **New tab** button [⊕], and then with the insertion point positioned in the **address bar** at the bottom of the screen, type **www.usmint.gov** and press [Enter] to display the website for **The United States Mint**.

8 In the **browsing window** for this site, point to the link **Learn** to display the [🖑] pointer, and then right-click. On the displayed menu, click **Open link in new tab**. Compare your screen with Figure 1.13.

Use this technique to open a link to a webpage in a separate tab without actually displaying the webpage. A tab for the Learn link is available but does not display, and the U.S. Mint homepage is still the active tab.

FIGURE 1.13

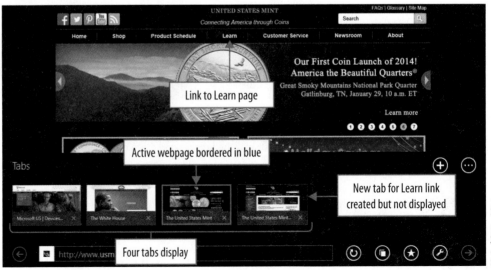

United States Mint

9 On the left side of the **tabs bar**, click the **Microsoft Home Page tab**.

In this manner, you can keep several websites open and move among them without having to retype the URL.

10 In the upper-right corner of the **tabs bar**, click the **New tab** button ⊕, and then with the insertion point positioned in the **address bar** at the bottom of the screen, type **www.supremecourt.gov** and press Enter to display the website for the **Supreme Court of the United States**.

11 Press Ctrl + T, which is the keyboard shortcut to open a new tab, and then type **www.bep.treas.gov** and press Enter to display the official site for the **Bureau of Engraving and Printing**.

12 By using either the **New tab** button ⊕ or the Ctrl + T technique, open the following three sites:

www.house.gov

www.senate.gov

www.state.gov

13 If necessary, point to an empty area of the **browsing window** to display the ⇱ pointer, right-click to display the **tabs bar**, and then compare your screen with Figure 1.14.

Depending on your screen's size and resolution, you may not be able to see all nine open tabs. To scroll the view of the tabs, point under the tabs to display a scroll bar, or by touch, swipe left or right under the row of tabs.

FIGURE 1.14

U.S. Department of State

14 To capture a screenshot of your **tabs bar**, hold down ⊞ and press PrintScrn. Notice that your screen dims momentarily.

15 Press ⊞ to display the **Start screen**, and then locate and click the **File Explorer** tile. If you do not see your File Explorer tile, with the Start screen displayed, type **file explorer** and then press Enter to start the app.

16 In the **This PC** window, double-click the **Pictures** folder, and then double-click the **Screenshots** folder to open it.

17 Click one time to select the Screenshot with the highest number. If necessary, in the upper-right corner, click ⌄ to expand the ribbon, and then on the **Home tab**, in the **Organize group**, click **Rename**. Using your own name, type **Lastname_Firstname_1A_Tabbed_Browsing** and press Enter.

18 With the newly renamed file still selected in the **file list**, in the **Clipboard group**, click **Copy**. From the **navigation pane**, if necessary expand This PC, and then open your USB drive. In the **New group**, click **New folder**. Name the folder **Internet Explorer 11 Chapter 1**

19 Open your **Internet Explorer 11 Chapter 1** folder, and then in the **Clipboard group**, click **Paste**. Hold this file until you have completed this project.

20 **Close** ⊠ the window, and then click the **Start button** ⊞ to redisplay the **Start screen**.

21 Click the **Internet Explorer** tile, and notice that your tabs still display.

> Because you did not close the app, all your tabs and the current webpage remain active.

22 On the last tab, for the **U.S. Department of State**, in the lower-right corner, click the **Close** button ×. Then, in the **tabs bar**, click the **Tab tools** button ☺. On the list, click **Reopen closed tab**.

> Use this technique to reopen a tab that you closed during your current browser session.

23 Right-click the active tab—bordered in blue—and click **Close other tabs**.

> Each open tab closes, and only the active webpage displays in the tabs bar.

24 Point to the top of the screen and on the right, click ┃ × ┃ to close the **Internet Explorer** app.

Objective 3 Search the Internet

The Internet can connect you to a vast amount of information, but first you have to find the information that you need. From Internet Explorer 11, you can search by typing a search term directly into the address bar.

Activity 1.03 │ Searching the Internet

A **search provider**—also called a **search engine**—is a website that provides search capabilities on the web. The default search provider in Internet Explorer is Microsoft's Bing. To search with Google, you can download and install the Google Search app from the Windows Store.

1 Display your **Start screen**. Point to the upper-left corner of your screen, and then move the mouse downward slightly to see if any apps are open. **Close** any open apps by right-clicking the open app tab and then clicking **Close**.

2 Click the **Internet Explorer** tile.

3 Click in the **address bar** to select the existing URL, type the search term "**washington dc tourism**" and then press Enter. Compare your screen with Figure 1.15.

> On the left, Bing displays suggested related links to websites, and in the list of results, words in your search term *washington dc tourism* display in bold. At the top, Bing displays **sponsored links**—paid advertisements shown as links, typically for products and services related to your search term. Sponsored links are the way that search sites such as Bing, Google, and others earn revenue.

> On the right, Bing displays information about Washington, DC.

> Placing quotation marks around your search term limits the search results to only those webpages that contain the exact phrase that you typed.

FIGURE 1.15

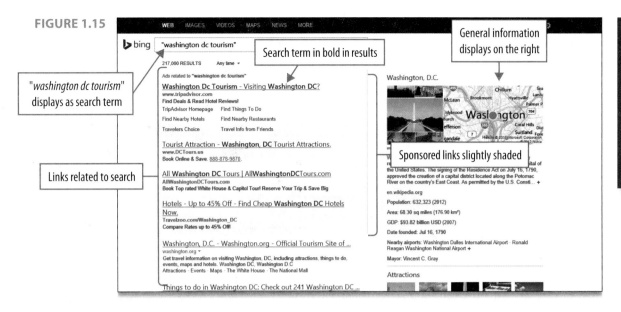

4 Take a moment to study the table in Figure 1.16 for advanced search options in Bing.

FIGURE 1.16

BING ADVANCED SEARCH OPTIONS	
Use This Symbol	**For This Function**
" "	Finds the exact words in a phrase that you type as a search term.
+	Finds webpages that contain all the terms that are preceded by the + symbol. Also enables you to include terms that are usually ignored.
( )	Finds or excludes webpages that contain a group of words.
AND or &	Finds webpages that contain all the terms or phrases.
NOT or –	Excludes webpages that contain a term or phrase.
OR or		Finds webpages that contain either of the terms or phrases.

Shelley Gaskin

5 Point to an empty area of the screen to display the pointer, and then right-click to display the **tabs bar**. Click the **New tab** button ⊕, and then in **address bar**, type **washington dc hotels** and press Enter.

6 Press Ctrl + T to open a new tab, and then in the **address bar**, search for **"washington dc memorials"**.

7 Press Ctrl + T to open a new tab, and then in the **address bar**, type **find washington dc chamber of commerce** and then press Enter. Compare your screen with Figure 1.17.

FIGURE 1.17

8 ▸ Point to an empty area of the screen to display the ⬚ pointer, and then right-click to display the **tabs bar**. Compare your screen with Figure 1.18.

> Four tabs with your four searches display. Use this technique when you are searching for multiple search terms to gather information so that you can switch among the sites you have targeted.

FIGURE 1.18

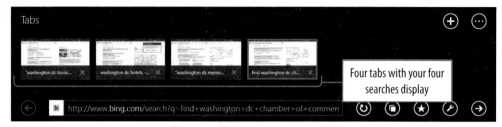

9 ▸ To capture a screenshot of your **tabs bar**, hold down ⊞ and press PrintScrn. Notice that your screen dims momentarily.

10 ▸ Press ⊞ to display the **Start screen**, and then locate and click the **File Explorer** tile. If you do not see your File Explorer tile, with the Start screen displayed, type **file explorer** and then click the app below the search box to start it.

11 ▸ In **This PC** window, double-click the **Pictures** folder, and then double-click the **Screenshots** folder to open it.

12 ▸ Click one time to select the Screenshot with the highest number, and then on the ribbon, in the **Organize group**, click **Rename**. Using your own name, type **Lastname_Firstname_1A_Four_Searches** and press Enter.

13 ▸ With the newly renamed file still selected in the **file list**, in the **Clipboard group**, click **Copy**. From the **navigation pane**, open your **USB drive**.

14 ▸ Open your **Internet Explorer 11 Chapter 1** folder, and then in the **Clipboard group**, click **Paste**. Hold this file until you have completed this project.

15 ▸ **Close** ⊠ the folder window, and then press ⊞ to redisplay the **Start screen**.

16 ▸ Click the **Internet Explorer** tile, and notice that your tabs still display.

> Because you did not close the app, all your tabs and current webpage remain active.

17 ▸ Point to the top of the screen and on the right, click ❌ to close the **Internet Explorer** app.

N O T E	**Printing a Webpage**

To print a webpage, with the webpage displayed, press Ctrl + P to display the Print pane on the right. Click the printer, adjust your settings, and then click Print.

Objective 4 | Browse with InPrivate

As you browse the web, Internet Explorer stores information about the websites you visit. It also stores information that you are frequently asked to provide. For example, if you type your name and address into a website, Internet Explorer stores that information. All this information is referred to as your **browsing history**.

Usually it is useful to have this information stored on your computer, because it speeds your web browsing and might automatically provide information so that you do not have to type it over and over.

Internet Explorer stores the following types of information:

- *Temporary Internet files*, which are copies of webpages, images, and media that you have downloaded from the web. Storing this information makes viewing faster the next time you visit a site that you have visited before.
- *Cookies*, which is the term used to refer to small text files that websites put on your computer to store information about you and your preferences, such as log-in information.
- A history of websites that you have visited.
- Information that you have entered into websites or the address bar, including your name and address if you have entered it into a site, and the URLs that you have visited before.
- Saved web passwords.

Activity 1.04 | Using InPrivate Browsing

Use *InPrivate Browsing* to browse the web without storing data about your browsing session. This feature is useful because it prevents anyone else who might be using your computer from seeing what sites you visited. By opening an InPrivate tab, websites that you visit in that tab along with passwords you enter, cookies you create, and temporary files that are downloaded are all deleted when you close the tab or close Internet Explorer.

Use this feature if you are browsing on a public computer, such as in your college labs or at a public library.

1 ▶ Display your **Start screen**. Point to the upper-left corner of your screen, and then move the mouse downward slightly to see if any apps are open. **Close** any open apps.

2 ▶ Click the **Internet Explorer** tile, point to an empty area of the screen to display the ⌖ pointer, and then right-click to display the **tabs bar**.

3 ▶ On the right side of the **tabs bar**, click **Tab tools** ⊙, and then click **New InPrivate tab**. Compare your screen with Figure 1.19.

A message indicates that InPrivate is turned on, and in the address bar, a blue icon indicates *InPrivate*. In this way, you know that your online activity is not being stored by the browser software.

FIGURE 1.19

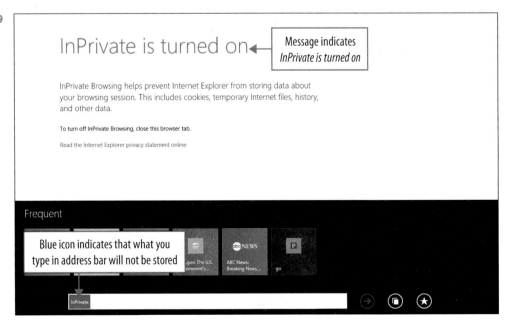

4 In the **address bar**, type **www.si.edu** and press $\boxed{\text{Enter}}$ to display the home page for the Smithsonian.

5 Click in the **address bar** to select the URL you just typed, and then type **www.gwu.edu/varsity-sports** Notice that InPrivate Browsing is still in effect, and then press $\boxed{\text{Enter}}$.

> While using InPrivate Browsing, Internet Explorer stores some information. For example, cookies are kept in memory so pages work properly but are cleared when you close the browser window. Temporary Internet files are also stored so pages work properly but are deleted when you close the browser window. Webpage history, form data, and passwords are not stored at all.

6 Point to the top of the screen and on the right, click $\boxed{\times}$ to close the **Internet Explorer** app.

> Cookies are cleared and temporary files are discarded.

Objective 5 | Configure Internet Explorer 11

From the Settings pane, you can configure Options for Internet Explorer 11.

Activity 1.05 | Configuring Internet Explorer 11

1 Display your **Start screen**, and then click the **Internet Explorer** tile.

2 Point to the upper-right corner of your screen to display the **charms**, and then click the **Settings** charm. Compare your screen with Figure 1.20.

FIGURE 1.20

3 In the **Settings pane**, click **Options**, and then scroll down as necessary to view the available options.

> Under Appearance, you can decide whether or not you would like the address bar and the tabs bar to always display. This may be useful if you frequently refer to the tabs displayed in the tabs bar, but you can use the $\boxed{\blacksquare}$+$\boxed{Z}$ keyboard shortcut to display tabs bar if you need to.
>
> Under Home pages, you can customize which sites, up to eight, to load on Internet Explorer 11 startup.
>
> Under Reading view, you can customize settings to your style and font preferences. You can choose from Bright, Medium, Light, and Dark style and Small, Medium, Large, and Extra Large fonts to make your reading view experience most enjoyable. When you find yourself in a different environment, you change these options, and they will immediately take effect on whatever site you are reading and will stay in effect until you change the setting.

Under Passwords, you can choose to have Internet Explorer offer to save your passwords when you log in to sites. You can Manage the sites for which Internet Explorer has stored your user names and passwords by viewing the Accounts. You can delete any password you no longer wish to be stored.

Under Phone numbers, you can choose to have Internet Explorer detect phone numbers on sites so that you may call them. With this option turned on, you can click a phone number and then select which app you would like to use to call.

The last setting is Fonts and encoding, which you will need only if you are visiting a website where the text is not displaying properly. This can occur with websites in other languages. In this setting, you can also change the reading direction.

Some settings take effect immediately; other settings require that the website be redisplayed for the setting to take effect.

4 Scroll as necessary, and then under **History**, click **Select**. Compare your screen with Figure 1.21.

Here you can choose which browsing data—such as cookies and browsing history—you want to delete from your PC. You can also choose to keep data for favorites when deleting history by setting the slider to On.

FIGURE 1.21

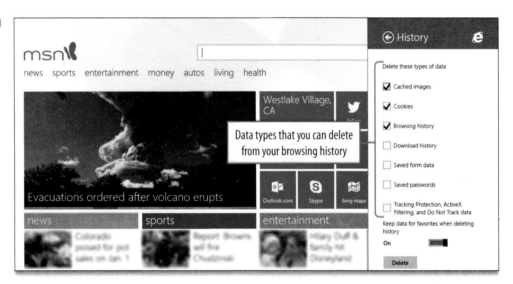

5 Click anywhere in the Internet Explorer screen outside of the pane to close the pane.

6 Point to the top of the screen and then on the right, click ☒ to close the **Internet Explorer** app.

END | You have completed Project 1A

Use Desktop Internet Explorer

PROJECT ACTIVITIES

In Activities 1.06 through 1.16, you will work with Barbara Hewitt and Steven Ramos, employees in the Information Technology Department at the headquarters office of Bell Orchid Hotels, as they explore how to browse and navigate the World Wide Web by using *Internet Explorer 11 in the desktop*. Bell Orchid Hotels is investigating a new hotel opportunity in Washington, DC, which will be geared to both business travelers and family vacations. Barbara and Steven have the assignment to conduct research on the web for this new hotel. You will capture screens that will look similar to Figure 1.22.

PROJECT FILES

For Project 1B, you will need the following files:

New Screenshot files

You will save your files as:

Lastname_Firstname_1B_Open_Tabs
Lastname_Firstname_1B_Favorites
Lastname_Firstname_1B_Print

PROJECT RESULTS

FIGURE 1.22 Project 1B Use Internet Explorer 11 in the Desktop

The desktop is the area in Windows 8.1 where you use desktop apps. In Windows 8.1, there are two versions of Internet Explorer 11—the touch friendly immersive app version that you practiced from the Start screen and the desktop version referred to as *Desktop Internet Explorer*. Both use the same underlying technologies, and both demonstrate quick startup, reliable performance, and adherence to the highest levels of web standards.

In Windows 8.1, both the Internet Explorer 11 app from the Start screen and the Desktop Internet Explorer 11 can run the Adobe Flash *plug-in*, which is a small program that adds capabilities to the browser such as playing video.

The decision as to which version of Internet Explorer 11 you use will depend on your device and your own preferences. On a touchscreen device such as a tablet, you will probably prefer to use the touch friendly version from the Start screen. If you spend most of your time using desktop apps with a mouse and keyboard, such as Microsoft Office, you will probably prefer to use Desktop Internet Explorer 11.

Activity 1.06 | Using Tabbed Browsing with Desktop Internet Explorer 11

1 Display your **desktop**, **Close** ☒ any open windows, and then on the taskbar, click **Internet Explorer** 🅔. Compare your screen with Figure 1.23, and then take a moment to study the table in Figure 1.24 that describes the parts of the Internet Explorer window.

If you have not set a home page, the default is usually a Microsoft site. Here Microsoft's site is shown as the home page.

On your computer, *home page* refers to whatever webpage you have selected—or is set by default—to display on your computer when you start Internet Explorer. When visiting a website, home page refers to the starting point for the remainder of the pages on that site.

For example, your computer manufacturer may have set its company site as the default home page. At your college, the home page of your college's website might be the home page on the computer at which you are working.

FIGURE 1.23

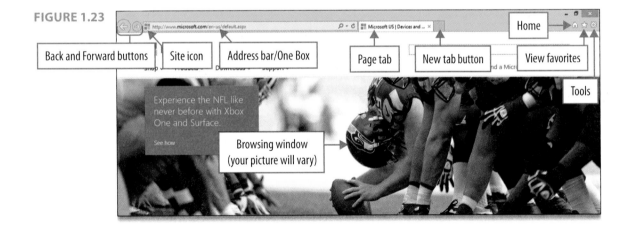

FIGURE 1.24

PARTS OF THE INTERNET EXPLORER IN THE DESKTOP SCREEN	
Screen Part	**Description**
Address bar	Provides the area in which you type the URL for the site you want to visit and which also works as a search box.
Back button	Displays the previous page you visited; activates after you visit more than one webpage.
Browsing window	Displays the webpage content for the site you are visiting.
Forward button	Displays the next page if you used the Back button.
Home button	Displays the website you have set as your home page.
New Tab button	Opens a new tab.
Page tab	Displays the name of the active webpage.
Site icon	Displays the icon of the website currently displayed in the browsing window; the Internet Explorer icon displays if IE 11 detects no icon for the site.
Tools button	Displays a menu from which you can access options for printing, security, zoom setting, and managing add-ons.
View favorites button	Displays a list of websites you have saved as favorites.

Shelley Gaskin

2 ▶ At the top of your screen, click in the **address bar** to select the current URL, type **usa.gov** and then press Enter.

If you completed Project 1A on the same computer, the autocomplete feature may fill in URLs for you, because the app version of Internet Explorer 11 that you used from the Start screen shares information and settings with the desktop version.

The address bar, based on the first few characters that you type, will search across your history and favorites displaying matches. When you see a match, click it to avoid retyping the entire URL of a site you have visited previously.

3 ▶ Click in the **address bar** to select the URL text, type **whitehouse.gov** and then press Enter.

Unless you open a new tab, a new URL opens its website on the first tab.

4 ▶ To the immediate right of the **Page tab** for **The White House**, point to the new tab to display the **New tab** button 🗔, and then click one time to open a new tab. Compare your screen with Figure 1.25.

A new tab opens. The White House website remains open on the previous tab. Tiles for sites that you visit frequently or visited recently display so that you can go to them quickly if you want to do so when you open a new tab.

More Knowledge   **To Set Your Home Page**

You can set one or more sites to open as your home page. To do so, display the site or group of sites that you want to set as your home page or home page group. Then point to a blank area above or to the right of the address bar, right-click, and if necessary, display the Command bar. On the Command bar, click the Home button arrow 🏠, click Add or change home page, and then select the appropriate option button. You can also click the Home button arrow to remove one or more sites from your Home group.

FIGURE 1.25

ANOTHER WAY   Press Ctrl + T to open a new tab.

5 ▶ With the insertion point blinking in the **address bar**, type **recreation.gov** and then press Enter to display the website for **Recreation.gov**.

6 ▶ Open new tabs for the following sites, and then compare your screen with Figure 1.26:

www.cr.nps.gov

www.usbg.gov

www.cfa.gov

FIGURE 1.26

U.S. Council of Fine Art

7 ▶ At the bottom of your screen, on the taskbar, *point* to the **Internet Explorer** icon 🅔 to display a thumbnail for each open tab. Compare your screen with Figure 1.27, and then leave these tabs open for the next activity.

Here you can see the websites that you have open in Internet Explorer, and you can navigate to a site by clicking its thumbnail image.

FIGURE 1.27

U.S. Council of Fine Art, Whitehouse, Recreation.gov, National Park Service

Activity 1.07 | Opening Links with Desktop Internet Explorer 11

1 Click the next to last tab, for the **United States Botanic Garden**, to display it in the **browsing window**. Locate the group of links for **ABOUT US, GARDENS, VISIT**, and so on, and then point to **GARDENS** to display the 🖑 pointer.

2 Press Ctrl + Shift, and then click the **GARDENS** link to open this webpage in a new tab. Compare your screen with Figure 1.28.

FIGURE 1.28

United States Botanic Garden

🔄 **ANOTHER WAY**   Point to the link, right-click, and then on the displayed menu, click Open in new tab.

3 Click the second tab for the **recreation.gov** site. On this page, locate and point to the link for **EXPLORE TRIP IDEAS** to display the 🖑 pointer, hold down Ctrl, and then click the **EXPLORE TRIP IDEAS** link. Notice that a new tab is created but does not open.

> Use this technique to open links in separate tabs without actually displaying them. When you are finished viewing the active page, you can investigate the other links you opened. Additionally, the tabs are colored to match so that you know they are related.

4 Click the tab for **The White House**, and then notice that the two tabs from the **recreation.gov** site are the same color. Compare your screen with Figure 1.29.

> When you open a link from a webpage, Internet Explorer 11 automatically includes them in a color-coded group.

FIGURE 1.29

Whitehouse

5 Point to either of the shaded tabs for the **recreation.gov** site, and then right-click to display a menu. Compare your screen with Figure 1.30. When tabs are in a group, you can use various commands to close the group or ungroup a tab from its group.

FIGURE 1.30

Whitehouse

6 At the bottom of the displayed menu, click **Show tabs on a separate row**, and then compare your screen with Figure 1.31.

> Some computer users prefer to show the address bar above the tabs row in this manner. If you typically have many tabs open, you might prefer this arrangement.

FIGURE 1.31

Tabs display on a separate row

7 To capture a screenshot, hold down [⊞] and press [PrintScrn]. Notice that your screen dims momentarily.

8 On the taskbar, click **File Explorer** [icon], and then in the **This PC** folder window, double-click the **Pictures** folder, and then double-click the **Screenshots** folder to open it.

9 Click one time to select the Screenshot with the highest number, and then on the ribbon, in the **Organize group**, click **Rename**. Using your own name, type **Lastname_Firstname_1B_ Open_Tabs** and press [Enter].

10 With the newly renamed file still selected in the **file list**, in the **Clipboard group**, click **Copy**. From the **navigation pane**, open your **USB drive**.

11 Open your **Internet Explorer 11 Chapter 1** folder, and then in the **Clipboard group**, click **Paste**. **Close** [×] the window. Hold this file until you have completed this project.

12 Point to any tab and right-click, and then click to deselect the **Show tabs on a separate row** command and restore to the default arrangement.

13 Point to **The White House** tab, right-click, and then click **Close other tabs**. Point to **The White House** tab again, and then click its **Close** button.

 ANOTHER WAY   Press [Ctrl] + [W] to close the active tab.

More **Knowledge**	**Cycling Through Open Tabs**
Hold down [Ctrl] and press [Tab] to cycle through and display all open tabs.	

Objective 7 | Organize Favorites and Manage Browsing History

The **Favorites Center** is a list of links to websites that is saved in your web browser. Saving a website as a favorite enables you to return to it quickly. For example, if you have a favorite health site that you visit frequently, you can save that site's address as a Favorite. Returning to the site requires only one or two clicks instead of typing a complete URL.

You can create a folder to organize your favorite links into groups that are meaningful to you. Then, you can either open one site from the folder or open all the sites in the folder with a single click.

Activity 1.08 | Organizing Favorites and Creating a Favorites Folder

In this activity, you will help Barbara and Steven organize a number of sites that they believe will be useful to those who are conducting research for the new hotel in Washington, DC.

1 **Close** [×] any open windows. On the taskbar, click **Internet Explorer** [icon], click in the **address bar**, type **house.gov** and then press [Enter].

2 Click the **New tab** button 📄, type **senate.gov** and then press ⏎.

Barbara and Steven know that one thing managers will be looking for is information about the popular locations that both tourists and business visitors will want to know about when they are guests at the hotel.

3 In the upper-right corner, click the **View favorites** button ⭐, and then at the top of the pane, to the right of *Add to Favorites*, click the ⏷ **arrow**. On the displayed list, click **Add current tabs to favorites**.

4 In the **Add Tabs to Favorites** dialog box, in the **Folder Name** box, type **Legislature** If necessary, click the Create in arrow and click Favorites. Compare your screen with Figure 1.32.

FIGURE 1.32

5 In the **Add Tabs to Favorites** dialog box, click **Add**. **Close** ❌ Internet Explorer, and then click **Close all tabs**.

6 Open **Internet Explorer** 🌐 again, and then in the upper-right corner, click the **View favorites** button ⭐. If necessary, at the top of the displayed list, click the Favorites tab. Click **Legislature** to expand the list, and then point to the arrow to the right of Legislature to display the ScreenTip. Compare your screen with Figure 1.33.

FIGURE 1.33

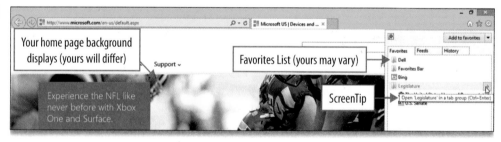

7 To the right of Legislature, click the **arrow** to open the entire group; notice that because they are in a group, the tabs are colored to match. Point to the tab for your home page, right-click, and then click **Close tab** so that only the two **Legislature tabs** display.

From the Favorites list, you can also click one of the links individually to open just one of the links.

8 Display the tab for the **U.S. Senate**, locate and point to the link for **VISITORS** to display the 👆 pointer, and then click the link. Then locate and click the link for **COMMITTEES**. If these links are not available, click another suitable link.

9 Click the **View favorites** button ⭐, click **Add to favorites**, and then in the **Add a Favorite** dialog box, click the **Create in arrow**. Compare your screen with Figure 1.34.

FIGURE 1.34

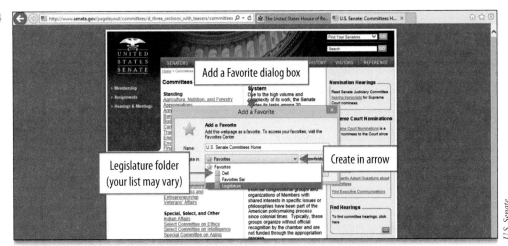

10 ▶ On the displayed list, click the **Legislature** folder, and then click the **Add** button.

The link is added to the folder *Legislature*.

11 ▶ **Close** 🗙 Internet Explorer, and then click **Close all tabs**.

Activity 1.09 | Using the Favorites Bar

You can display a ***Favorites bar***, which is a toolbar that displays directly below the address bar and to which you can add or drag web addresses you use frequently.

1 ▶ On the taskbar, click **Internet Explorer** 🅴. Point to an empty area above or to the right of the **address bar**, right-click, and then compare your screen with Figure 1.35.

FIGURE 1.35

2 ▶ On the menu, click **Favorites bar**, and then notice the **Favorites bar** under your **address bar**.

3 ▶ Click in the **address bar** to select the existing URL, type **weather.gov** and then press ⏎.

4 ▶ Directly below the **address bar**, click the **Add to Favorites bar** button 📄. Compare your screen with Figure 1.36.

FIGURE 1.36

5 Click in the **address bar**, type **visitthecapitol.gov** and press `Enter`. At the left end of the **address bar**, point to the **Capitol building logo**, hold down the left mouse button, and then drag the logo onto the **Favorites bar** until a black line displays to the right of the NOAA's site, as shown in Figure 1.37.

FIGURE 1.37

6 On the **Favorites bar**, point to the **National Weather Service** site, right-click, and then click **Rename**. In the **Rename** dialog box, type **NOAA** and then click **OK**. Using the same technique, rename *U.S. Capitol Visitor Center* link to **US Capitol** Compare your screen with Figure 1.38.

> You can change and shorten the names on your Favorites bar to make additional space. When you have more Favorites than the bar can accommodate, double chevrons will display at the right, which when clicked will display a continuation of the list.

FIGURE 1.38

7 Click in the **address bar**, type **www.archives.gov** and press `Enter`, and then drag its logo to the **Favorites bar** to the right of **US Capitol**.

8 To capture a screenshot, hold down 🪟 and press `PrintScrn`. Notice that your screen dims momentarily.

9 On the taskbar, click **File Explorer** 🗂, and then in **This PC** window, double-click the **Pictures** folder, and then double-click the **Screenshots** folder to open it.

10 Click one time to select the Screenshot with the highest number, and then on the ribbon, in the **Organize group**, click **Rename**. Using your own name, type **Lastname_Firstname_1B_Favorites** and press `Enter`.

11 With the newly renamed file still selected in the **file list**, in the **Clipboard group**, click **Copy**. From the **navigation pane**, open your **USB drive**.

12 Open your **Internet Explorer 11 Chapter 1** folder, and then in the **Clipboard group**, click **Paste**. **Close** ☒ the folder window. Hold this file until you have completed this project.

13 Point to the **National Archives** link on the **Favorites bar**, right-click, and then click **Delete**. By using the same technique, delete the links for the **US Capitol** and **NOAA**.

14 **Close** ☒ Internet Explorer.

> On your own computer, if you want to do so, display the Favorites bar and place links to the sites you use most frequently on it. For other favorite sites, add them to the Favorites Center.

Activity 1.10 | Viewing and Deleting Browsing History

Recall that as you browse the web, Internet Explorer stores information about the websites you visit. This is referred to as your browsing history. You can view and delete your browsing history while using the desktop version of Internet Explorer 11.

1 On the taskbar, click **Internet Explorer** . Click the **View favorites** button , and then at the top of the pane, click the **History tab**. Under **History**, click the **arrow**, and then if necessary, click View By Date. Click **Today**. Click the **arrow** to display the list again, click **View By Order Visited Today**, and then compare your screen with Figure 1.39.

Here you can view a list of the sites you visited today.

FIGURE 1.39

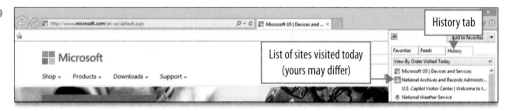

2 To the right or above the **address bar**, right-click, and then click **Command bar** to display this toolbar. On the **Command bar**, click **Safety**.

Here you can select InPrivate Browsing in the same manner you practiced using Internet Explorer from the Start screen.

3 Click **Delete browsing history**.

Here you can delete all your web browsing history, or individually select one or more categories of data, files, sites, and passwords to delete.

4 Unless you are working on your own computer and you do not want to delete any files, click the **Delete** button, and then wait a few moments for the deletion to complete.

Deleting all browsing history does not delete your list of Favorites. This action deletes only temporary files, your browsing history, cookies, and saved form information passwords—if their checkboxes are selected.

If you perform this action on your own computer, it might take a few seconds longer to display sites again the first time you access them. After that, the system will rebuild your browsing history as you browse the web.

5 **Close** Internet Explorer.

More Knowledge | **Close Internet Explorer After Deleting Browser History**

Close Internet Explorer after deleting your browser history to clear cookies that are still in memory from your current browsing session. This is especially important when using a public computer such as in your college computer lab.

The Page Zoom feature enables you to increase or decrease the page size for easier viewing. You can also adjust the size of displayed text.

Activity 1.11 | Printing Webpages

Internet Explorer 11 provides useful options for formatting and then printing a webpage. In the following activity, you will work with Barbara and Steven to print a webpage.

1 ▶ **Close** ☒ any open windows. On the taskbar, click **Internet Explorer** 🅔, click in the **address bar**, type **usa.gov** and then press ⏎. Click the link for **Government Agencies**.

The site **usa.gov**, which serves as the official *portal* for the U.S. government, displays. A portal is a website that displays news, content, and links that are of interest to a specific audience; for example, individuals who need information about government agencies and services.

2 ▶ On the **Command bar**, locate and click the **Print button arrow** 🖶 to display a menu. Compare your screen with Figure 1.40.

FIGURE 1.40

3 ▶ On the menu, click **Print preview**. Compare your screen with Figure 1.41, and then take a moment to study the parts of the Print Preview window described in the table in Figure 1.42.

Recall that Internet Explorer will shrink the page as necessary to fit horizontally on the selected paper size. You can also drag the margins by using the adjust margin buttons on this Print Preview screen.

FIGURE 1.41

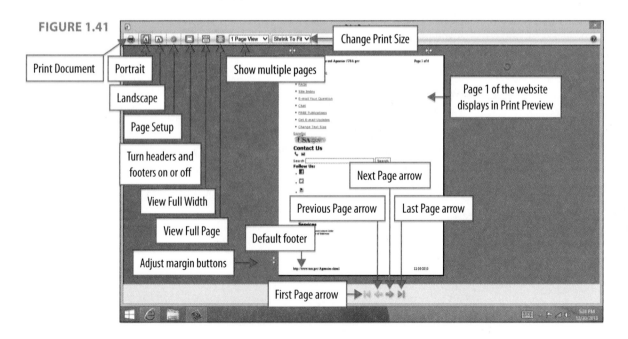

FIGURE 1.42

PARTS OF THE PRINT PREVIEW WINDOW IN INTERNET EXPLORER 11	
Adjust margin buttons	Adjusts the left, right, top, and bottom margins by dragging.
Change Print Size	Stretches or shrinks the page size to fill the printed page.
First Page arrow	Displays the first page of multiple pages in the preview screen.
Landscape	Prints the page in landscape orientation, in which the paper is wider than it is tall.
Last Page arrow	Displays the last page of multiple pages in the preview screen.
Next Page arrow	Displays the next page of multiple pages in the preview screen.
Page indicator	Indicates the page displayed and the total number of pages.
Page Setup	Opens the Page Setup dialog box, in which you can change paper size, orientation, margins, font, and header and footer options.
Portrait	Prints the page in portrait orientation, in which the paper is taller than it is wide.
Previous Page arrow	Displays the previous page of multiple pages in the preview screen.
Print Document	Opens the Print dialog box, enabling you to print the page using the current settings.
Show multiple pages	Displays multiple pages on the preview screen.
Turn headers or footers on or off	Turns the display of headers and footers on or off in the manner of a toggle button.
View Full Page	Zooms the webpage to show the full webpage in the preview screen.
View Full Width	Zooms the webpage to the width of the preview screen.

Shelley Gaskin

4 On the **Print Preview Command bar**, click the **Show multiple pages arrow** ▾, and then click **2 Page View**.

5 On the **Command bar**, to the right of *Shrink To Fit*, click the **Change Print Size button arrow** ▾, and then on the displayed list, click **Custom**. In the % box, type **85** and press Enter. Compare your screen with Figure 1.43.

FIGURE 1.43

 ANOTHER WAY   Experiment with percentages on the list, or by typing in the Custom box, to shrink the page to print the way you want it to—on one or more pages.

6 On the **Command bar**, to the right of *2 Page View*, click the **Show multiple pages button arrow** ▾, and then click **1 Page View** to return to that view and center the page on the Print Preview screen.

7 On the **Command bar**, click the **Page Setup** button ⊙. Compare your screen with Figure 1.44.

Here you can change or add to the headers and footers on a printed webpage.

By default there are two headers, one left aligned and one right aligned, which will display the page title and the Page # of total pages. Similarly, there are two footers, one left aligned and one right aligned, which will display the URL and the date in short format.

The default setting for the centered header and footer is *Empty*. You can change any of the headers and footers by clicking the arrow and selecting an item or by selecting Custom and creating a new entry. You can also change the font of the headers and footers.

FIGURE 1.44

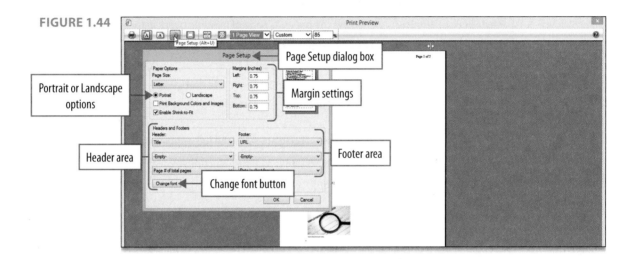

8 Under **Footer**, click the second arrow, and then click **Custom**.

Here you can enter a centered footer.

9 In the **Custom** dialog box, using your own name, type **Firstname Lastname** and then click **OK**. In the **Page Setup** dialog box, click **OK**.

In the Print Preview screen, your name displays as a centered heading.

10 To capture a screenshot, hold down 🪟 and press PrintScrn. Notice that your screen dims momentarily.

11 On the taskbar, click **File Explorer** 📁, and then in **This PC** window, double-click the **Pictures** folder and then double-click the **Screenshots** folder to open it.

12 Click one time to select the Screenshot with the highest number, and then on the ribbon, in the **Organize group**, click **Rename**. Using your own name, type **Lastname_Firstname_1B_Print** and press Enter.

13 With the newly renamed file still selected in the **file list**, in the **Clipboard group**, click **Copy**. From the **navigation pane**, open your **USB drive**.

14 Open your **Internet Explorer 11 Chapter 1** folder, and then in the **Clipboard group**, click **Paste**. **Close** the folder window. Hold this file until you have completed this project.

15 **Close** the **Print Preview** screen, and then **Close** Internet Explorer.

More Knowledge	Printing Specific Parts of a Webpage

To print only a specific part of a webpage, use your mouse to select the content that you want to print. Click the Print button arrow, click Print, and then in the Print dialog box, click the Selection option button. Click Print.

Activity 1.12 | Zooming and Changing the Text Size of Webpages

1 ▶ **Close** [×] any open windows. On the taskbar, click **Internet Explorer** 🟦, click in the **address bar**, type **senate.gov** and press Enter. On the **Command bar**, click the **Page** button, point to **Zoom**, and then click **200%**.

> The view of the page is increased to 200%. Increasing the Zoom level increases the size of everything on the page, including graphics and controls.

2 ▶ Using the technique you just practiced, change the **Zoom** level to **50%**.

3 ▶ Hold down Ctrl and then roll your mouse wheel backward and forward to increase and decrease the zoom.

> This is a useful technique if you want to briefly magnify some text that is difficult to read or to examine a photo closely.

4 ▶ Change the **Zoom** level back to **100%**.

5 ▶ Open a **New Tab** 🗋, type **www.archives.gov** and then press Enter. On the **Command bar**, click the **Page** button, and then point to **Text size**.

> The default text size is Medium, but if you would like to see more text on the screen, you can set a smaller text size. If you have difficulty reading webpages on your screen, you can set a larger text size.

> Changing the text size affects only the text—graphics and controls continue to display in their original size.

6 ▶ On the displayed submenu, click **Largest**, and notice that the text on your screen is enlarged. Compare your screen with Figure 1.45.

FIGURE 1.45

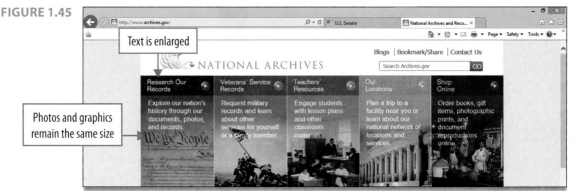

7 ▶ Using the technique you just practiced, return the **Text Size** to **Medium**.

8 ▶ **Close** 🟦 Internet Explorer.

NOTE	The Text Size of Some Webpages Is Set by the Person Who Created the Page

The creator of the webpage may set a specific text size that you cannot change with the Text size command. If you want to do so, you can override as follows: click the Tools button on the Command bar, click Internet options, on the General tab, click the Accessibility button, and then select the Ignore font sizes specified on webpages checkbox.

Objective 9 | Save Webpage Information

You can save an entire webpage, an image on a webpage, or selected text from a webpage. Doing so is a good way to capture information to which you want to refer to later without accessing the Internet.

Activity 1.13 | Saving Webpage Information

1 **Close** [✕] any open windows. On the taskbar, click **Internet Explorer** [e], click in the **address bar**, type **nga.gov** and then press [Enter].

2 On the **Command bar**, click the **Page** button, and then click **Save as**. At the bottom of the displayed **Save Webpage** dialog box, click the **Save as type arrow**, and then compare your screen with Figure 1.46.

To save all files associated with the page, including graphics, frames, and style sheets in their original format, you can use the file format *Webpage, complete (*.htm;*.html)*.

To save all information as a single file, you can use the file format *Web Archive, single file (*.mht)*.

To save just the current HTML page, without graphics, sounds, or other files, you can use the file format *Webpage, HTML only (*.htm;*.html)*.

To save just the text from the current webpage, you can use the file format *Text File (*.txt)*.

FIGURE 1.46

National Gallery of Art

3 ▶ **Close** ⊠ the **Save Webpage** dialog box without saving, and then **Close** ⊠ Internet Explorer.

More Knowledge   **Emailing a Webpage**

You can email a webpage in two ways. From the Page button menu, click Send page by e-mail or click Send link by e-mail. Your default email program will display. The first option inserts the entire page in the text of the email message. The second option inserts only the URL in the text of the email message.

To set a program to use for email within Internet Explorer, on the Command bar, click the Tools button, click Internet options, click the Programs tab, and then under Internet programs, click the Set programs button.

Objective 10   Protect Your Data

Windows 8.1 and Internet Explorer 11 provide a variety of ways to protect your personal data and your electronic transactions.

Activity 1.14 │ Using the Internet Explorer 11 Pop-up Blocker and Information Bar

A *pop-up* is a small web browser window that displays on top of the website you are viewing; pop-ups are usually created by advertisers. *Pop-up blocker* is a feature in Internet Explorer that enables you to limit or block most pop-ups. The Notification bar displays information about downloads, blocked pop-up windows, and other activities. Pop-up blocker is enabled by default. To turn it off or change the settings, display the Tools menu, as shown in Figure 1.47.

FIGURE 1.47

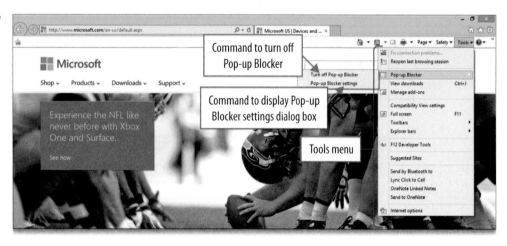

By displaying the Pop-up Blocker Settings dialog box, you can *allow* pop-ups from specific websites, as shown in Figure 1.48. You can also select the Blocking level and decide whether to play a sound or show the Notification bar when a pop-up is blocked. These default settings are appropriate for most computer users. Some sites request that you allow pop-ups from their site, and if you trust the site, it is safe to do so.

Because the Notification bar displays on a site when a pop-up is blocked, you always have the choice of viewing the pop-up message if you want to do so. Click the Notification bar and then click Show Blocked Pop-up. From the Notification bar, you can also click to temporarily accept pop-ups from a specific site.

FIGURE 1.48

The Notification bar will display if:

- A site tries to install an ActiveX control, install an updated ActiveX control, install an add-on program, run an ActiveX control in an unsafe manner, or run active content.
- A site tries to download a file to your computer.
- Your security settings are below the recommended levels.
- You started Internet Explorer with add-ons disabled.

One advantage of the Notification bar is that you are not required to attend to it. For example, if you display a site by mistakenly typing an incorrect URL, you can ignore the Notification bar. If you want to proceed with using a feature of the displayed site, click the message and then take appropriate action.

To check how well you can identify pop-up blocking functions, take a moment to answer the following questions:

1 By default, pop-up blocker is _____.

2 You always have the choice of _____ a pop-up message if you want to do so.

3 One common reason that the Notification bar will display is if a website tries to install, update, or run in an unsafe manner any type of _____ control.

4 The Notification bar commonly displays if a site tries to _____ a file to your computer.

5 One advantage of the Notification bar is that you are not _____ to do anything with it.

Activity 1.15 | Protecting Against Malware

Internet Explorer will warn you when webpages try to install software by displaying the Notification bar. There are additional ways in which Internet Explorer provides safety features to protect your computer against malware.

Internet Explorer's **protected mode** makes it more difficult for malicious software to be installed on your computer by preventing a downloaded program from making any direct changes to the system. It also allows you to install *wanted* ActiveX controls or add-ons when you are logged in as an administrator. Protected mode is on by default, and you will see it indicated in the status bar. One way that protected mode helps protect your computer from malicious downloads is by restricting where files can be saved without your consent.

Windows Defender is a spyware scanning and removal tool included with Windows 8.1. By default, Windows Defender, when enabled, scans your computer for spyware automatically daily. During the scan, Windows Defender takes automatic action on various items, depending on your preferences. If any spyware is found, you are prompted with options to deal with each threat by selecting Ignore, Quarantine, Remove, or Always Allow. Windows Defender constantly updates its definitions so that it can find new spyware threats that emerge on the Internet.

The first step in using Windows Defender is to make sure it is enabled on your computer. To do so, open the Control Panel by right-clicking the Start button (need to create an icon for this) and click Control Panel and then click Windows Defender. If you do not see Windows Defender displayed in the list, type *windows defender* in the search box and access it in this manner. To enable or change the settings of Windows Defender, click the Settings tab, as shown in Figure 1.49.

FIGURE 1.49

Activity 1.16 | Protecting Your Data

A *certificate* is a digital document that verifies the identity of a person or indicates the security of a website. Certificates are issued by trusted companies known as *certification authorities*. Certificates make secure transactions on the Internet possible. When you visit a secure website in Internet Explorer, a padlock icon will display in the address bar indicating that a digital certificate identifies the site. As shown in Figure 1.50, you can click the padlock icon to display information about the certificate.

FIGURE 1.50

National Gallery of Art

You can see specific information about the issuer of the certificate by clicking *View certificates*. You will commonly see such certificate information on any site where financial transactions are involved.

Phishing is a technique used to trick computer users into revealing personal or financial information through an email message or a website. The message or site appears to come from a trusted source but actually directs recipients to provide information to a fraudulent website.

SmartScreen Filter is a feature in Internet Explorer that helps detect phishing websites and websites that distribute malware. SmartScreen Filter runs in the background and protects you by comparing the addresses of websites you visit against a list of sites reported to Microsoft as legitimate. This list is stored on your computer. It also analyzes the sites you visit to see if they have characteristics common to a phishing site.

To manually check a website that you find suspicious, navigate to the site you want to check, on the Command bar, click Safety, point to SmartScreen Filter, click Check this website, and then click OK. If a website is flagged as suspicious, you should not submit any personal or financial information to it unless you are certain that the site is trustworthy. Suspicious sites are flagged by Internet Explorer by displaying the address bar in yellow along with a message. For more information about how Internet Explorer handles data protection, in the Windows Help and Support window, click on Security, privacy, & accounts.

Another feature in Internet Explorer 11 is **Do Not Track**, which sends a signal to websites that you prefer not to have information about your visit used in a manner to track you as you browse the web.

To check how well you understand data and family protection, take a moment to answer the following questions:

1 A certificate can verify the _____ of a website.

2 Certificates make _____ transactions on the web possible.

3 When you visit a secure website, the address bar displays a _____ icon.

4 A technique to trick computer users into revealing personal information is _____.

5 If the SmartScreen Filter in Internet Explorer suspects a website of having phishing characteristics, it will display a message and display the address bar in _____.

END | You have completed Project 1B

END OF CHAPTER

SUMMARY

Browsing with Internet Explorer from the Windows 8.1 Start screen is optimized for touch and distraction-free browsing. Tabbed browsing enables you to open multiple websites while researching a project. Internet Explorer 11 includes features to make reading, printing, and saving webpages easy. You can pin Favorites to the Start screen for instant access and notifications. Keep your web browsing safe and private to protect your data.

A search provider—or search engine—provides search capabilities on the web. The default search provider in Internet Explorer 11 is Microsoft's Bing, and you can also install the Google Search app to search with Google.

Internet Explorer stores information about websites you visit. Use InPrivate Browsing to browse without any information being stored. By opening an InPrivate tab, information is deleted when you close the tab.

Internet Explorer 11 has two versions—the Start screen app version and the desktop app version. Use whichever version is convenient and comfortable for you. Both programs share the same information and underlying technology.

GO! LEARN IT ONLINE

Review the concepts and key terms in this chapter by completing these online challenges, which you can find at **www.pearsonhighered.com/go**.

Matching and Multiple Choice:
Answer matching and multiple choice questions to test what you learned in this chapter. MyITLab®

END OF CHAPTER

REVIEW AND ASSESSMENT GUIDE FOR INTERNET EXPLORER 11 CHAPTER 1

Your instructor may assign one or more of these projects to help you review the chapter and assess your mastery and understanding of the chapter.

	Review and Assessment Guide for Internet Explorer 11 Chapter 1		
Project	**Apply Skills from These Chapter Objectives**	**Project Type**	**Project Location**
1C	Objectives 1–5 from Project 1A	**1C Skills Review** A guided review of the skills from Project 1A.	On the following pages
1D	Objectives 6–10 from Project 1B	**1D Skills Review** A guided review of the skills from Project 1B.	On the following pages
1E	Objectives 1–5 from Project 1A	**1E Mastery** A demonstration of your mastery of the skills in Project 1A with decision making.	On the following pages
1F	Objectives 6–10 from Project 1B	**1F Mastery** A demonstration of your mastery of the skills in Project 1B with decision making.	On the following pages
1G	Combination of Objectives from Projects 1A and 1B	**1G GO! Think** A demonstration of your understanding of the chapter concepts applied in a manner that you would outside of college. An analytic rubric helps you and your instructor grade the quality of your work by comparing it to the work an expert in the discipline would create.	On the following pages
1H	Combination of Objectives from Projects 1A and 1B	**1H GO! Think** A demonstration of your understanding of the chapter concepts applied in a manner that you would outside of college. An analytic rubric helps you and your instructor grade the quality of your work by comparing it to the work an expert in the discipline would create.	On the following pages
1I	Combination of Objectives from Projects 1A and 1B	**1I GO! Think** A demonstration of your understanding of the chapter concepts applied in a manner that you would outside of college. An analytic rubric helps you and your instructor grade the quality of your work by comparing it to the work an expert in the discipline would create.	On the following pages

GLOSSARY

GLOSSARY OF CHAPTER KEY TERMS

Address bar In Internet Explorer 11, the area in which you can type a URL to visit a website; displays at the bottom of the screen in the Start screen version of IE 11 and at the top of the screen in the desktop version of IE 11.

Blog An online journal or column used to publish personal or company information in an informal manner.

Browsing The term used to describe the process of using your computer to view webpages.

Browsing history The information stored by Internet Explorer about the sites you have visited and the information you have typed into a site.

Browsing window In Internet Explorer 11, the area of the screen in which the webpage displays.

Certificate A digital document that verifies the identity of a person or indicates the security of a website.

Certification authorities Companies, such as VeriSign, that issue digital certificates.

Cookies Small text files that websites put on your computer to store information about you and your preferences, such as log-in information.

Country codes Top-level domains for countries, such as *.ca* for Canada.

Desktop Internet Explorer In Windows 8.1, a version of Internet Explorer 11.

Do Not Track A feature in Internet Explorer 11 that sends a signal to websites that you prefer not to have information about your visit used in a manner to track you as you browse the web.

Domain name An organization's unique name on the Internet, which consists of a chosen name combined with a top-level domain such as **.com**, **.org**, or **.gov**.

Favorites bar A toolbar in Internet Explorer 11 that you can optionally display directly above the address bar in the Start screen version and directly below the address bar in the desktop version and to which you can add or drag web addresses you use frequently.

Favorites Center A list of links to websites that is saved in your web browser.

Flip ahead Enables you to swipe across the page to move to the next page of content.

Home page On your own computer, the webpage you have selected—or that is set by default—to display on your computer when you start Internet Explorer; when visiting a website, the starting point for the remainder of the pages on that site.

http The protocol prefix for HyperText Transfer Protocol.

HyperText Transfer Protocol The set of communication rules used by your computer to connect to servers on the web.

IE 11 The acronym for Internet Explorer 11.

InPrivate Browsing A feature in Internet Explorer 11 with which you can browse the web without storing data about your browsing session; useful when using a public computer.

Internet Explorer 11 The web browser software developed by Microsoft Corporation that is included with Windows 8.1; there are two versions that use the same underlying information and technology—one version for the Start screen and one version for the desktop.

Internet Explorer 11 in the desktop The term for the version of Internet Explorer 11 used on the desktop.

Phishing A technique used to trick computer users into revealing personal or financial information through an email message or a website.

Plug-ins Small programs that add capabilities to the browser software such as playing video or scanning for viruses.

Pop-up A small web browser window that displays on top of the website you are viewing, and which is usually created by advertisers.

Pop-up blocker A feature in Internet Explorer that enables you to block most pop-ups.

Portal A website that displays news, content, and links that are of interest to a specific audience.

Protected mode A feature in Internet Explorer that makes it more difficult for malicious software to be installed on your computer by preventing a downloaded program from making any direct changes to the system.

Protocol prefix The letters that represent a set of communication rules used by a computer to connect to another computer.

Search engine A computer program that searches for specific words and returns a list of documents in which the search term was found.

Search provider A website that provides search capabilities on the web.

SmartScreen Filter A feature in Internet Explorer that helps detect phishing websites and websites that distribute malware.

Sponsored links Paid advertisements shown as links, typically for products and services related to your search term.

Surfing The process of navigating the Internet either for a particular item or for anything that is of interest and quickly moving from one item to another.

Tabbed browsing A feature in Internet Explorer that enables you to open multiple websites and then switch among them.

Tabs bar In Internet Explorer 11, the bar that displays a tab for each webpage that you currently have open.

Temporary Internet files Copies of webpages, images, and media that you have downloaded from the web, which makes viewing faster the next time you visit a site that you have visited before.

TLD The acronym for top-level domain.

Top-level domain The ending letters of a URL such as .com, .org, and .gov.

Uniform resource locator An address that uniquely identifies a location on the Internet.

URL The acronym for uniform resource locator.

Web browser A software program with which you display webpages and navigate the Internet.

Web log The term from which *blog* is derived; an online journal or column used to publish personal or company information in an informal manner.

Windows Defender A spyware scanning and removal tool included with Windows 8.1.

CHAPTER REVIEW

Apply 1A skills from these Objectives:

1 Navigate with Internet Explorer 11

2 Navigate with Tabs

3 Search the Internet

4 Browse with InPrivate

5 Configure Internet Explorer 11

Skills Review   Project 1C Navigate Internet Explorer 11

PROJECT FILES

For Project 1C, you will need the following files:

Your USB flash drive containing the student data files

ie01_1C_Answer_Sheet (Word document)

You will save your file as:

LastnameFirstname_1C_Answer_Sheet

1 Display the **Start screen**; point to the upper-left corner, and then **Close** any open apps. Display the **desktop. Close** ☒ any open desktop windows. On the taskbar, click **File Explorer**. In the **navigation pane**, click your **USB drive** that contains the student files for this textbook, and then navigate to **Chapter_Files** ▶**Chapter_01**. Double-click the Word file **ie01_1C_Answer_Sheet** to open Word and display the document. If necessary, at the top, click Enable editing; be sure the window is maximized. In the upper-left corner, click **FILE**, click **Save As**, click **Computer**, and then click **Browse** to display the **Save As** dialog box. In the **navigation pane**, click your **USB drive**, and then double-click to open your **Internet Explorer 11_Chapter_1** folder. Using your own name, **Save** the document as **Lastname_Firstname_1C_Answer_Sheet** Click **Save**.

On the taskbar, click the **Word** button to minimize the window and leave your Word document accessible from the taskbar. **Close** the **Chapter_1** folder window. As you complete each step in this project, write the letter of your answer on a piece of paper; you will fill in your answer sheet after you complete all the steps in this project.

Display the **Start screen**, and then click the **Internet Explorer** tile. In the **address bar**, click the existing URL to select it, type **microsoft.com** and then press Enter. Which of the following is *not* true?

A.   From this screen, you can add this site to your Favorites.

B.   From this screen, you can go back to the previous webpage that was displayed.

C.   From this screen, you can go forward to the next webpage of content.

2 In the **address bar**, click the existing URL, type **usa.gov** and then press Enter. What is the term used to describe the area in which the information about the government displays?

A.   web window

B.   browsing window

C.   app window

3 In the **address bar**, which of the following identifies this site's top-level domain?

A.   .gov

B.   usa

C.   http

4 Click the URL in the **address bar**, type **weather.gov** and then press Enter. In the **browsing window**, point to the left-center edge of the screen, and then click ◀. What is your result?

A.   The webpage for bing.com displays.

B.   The webpage for microsoft.com displays.

C.   The webpage for usa.gov displays.

(Project 1C Navigate Internet Explorer 11 continues on the next page)

CHAPTER REVIEW

5 Point to an empty area of the **browsing window** to display the ▨ pointer, and then right-click. What is your result?

A. The address bar displays at the bottom of the screen.

B. The tabs bar displays above the address bar.

C. Both A and B.

6 In the **tabs bar**, click the **New tab** button ⊕. Which of the following is *not* true?

A. The browsing window is empty.

B. A message displays prompting you to type a URL.

C. The insertion point is blinking in the address bar at the bottom of the screen.

7 In the **address bar**, type **nyc.gov/visitors** and press Enter. When the webpage displays, press Ctrl + T to open a new tab, and then type **radiocity.com** and press Enter. Press Ctrl + T to open a new tab, and then type **iloveny.com** and press Enter. Point to an empty area of the **browsing window** to display the ▨ pointer, and then right-click. Which of the following is true?

A. Five tabs display in the tabs bar.

B. Four tabs display in the tabs bar.

C. Three tabs display in the tabs bar.

8 In the **tabs bar**, click the tab for **Radio City Music Hall**. Locate the link **GET TICKETS**, point to the link to display the ▨ pointer, right-click, and then click **Open link in new tab**. Which of the following is true?

A. A tab for a Calendar of Events for Radio City Music Hall displays in the tabs bar.

B. The webpage for I Love NY displays in the browsing window.

C. The **usa.gov** tab is the active tab.

9 On the **tabs bar**, click the **Tab tools** button ☺, and then click **New InPrivate tab**. Which of the following is *not* true?

A. A blue icon labeled *InPrivate* displays in the address bar.

B. The box to type a URL is empty.

C. The microsoft.com site displays in the browsing window.

10 As the URL, type **amazon.com** and press Enter. Which of the following is *not* true?

A. Anyone who uses your computer will not be able to see that you visited the amazon.com website.

B. Any cookies created by visiting amazon.com will be deleted when you close Internet Explorer.

C. You will not be able to make a purchase at amazon.com because you initiated InPrivate Browsing.

    To complete this project: Point to the top edge of the screen and on the right, click ☒ to close **Internet Explorer**. Be sure your desktop displays. On the taskbar, click the **Word** button, and then type your answers into the correct boxes. **Save** and **close** your Word document, and submit as directed by your instructor. **Close** all open windows.

> **END | You have completed Project 1C**

CHAPTER REVIEW

Apply 1B skills from these Objectives:

6 Use Desktop Internet Explorer 11

7 Organize Favorites and Manage Browsing History

8 Print, Zoom, and Change the Text Size of Webpages

9 Save Webpage Information

10 Protect Your Data

Skills Review | Project 1D Use Desktop Internet Explorer 11

PROJECT FILES

For Project 1D, you will need the following files:

Your USB flash drive containing the student data files

ie01_1D_Answer_Sheet (Word document)

You will save your file as:

Lastname_Firstname_1D_Answer_Sheet

1 Display the **Start screen**; point to the upper-left corner, and then **Close** any open apps. Display the **desktop**. **Close** ☒ any open desktop windows. On the taskbar, click **File Explorer**. In the **navigation pane**, click your **USB drive** that contains the student files for this textbook, and then navigate to **Chapter_Files ▶Chapter_01**. Double-click the Word file **ie01_1D_Answer_Sheet** to open Word and display the document. If necessary, at the top, click Enable editing; be sure the window is maximized. In the upper-left corner, click **FILE**, click **Save As**, click **Computer**, and then click **Browse** to display the **Save As** dialog box. In the **navigation pane**, click your **USB drive**, and then double-click to open your **Internet Explorer 11 Chapter 1** folder. Using your own name, **Save** the document as **Lastname_Firstname_1D_Answer_Sheet** Click **Save**.

On the taskbar, click the **Word** button to minimize the window and leave your Word document accessible from the taskbar. **Close** the **Chapter_01** folder window. As you complete each step in this project, write the letter of your answer on a piece of paper; you will fill in your answer sheet after you complete all the steps in this project.

From the taskbar on the desktop, click **Internet Explorer**. Be sure that you have displayed the **Favorites bar** and the **Command bar**. Click in the **address bar** and navigate to **doh.state.fl.us**. Open a New tab, and then go to the site **miamigov.com**. Which of the following is true?

A. The tabs display in alphabetical order by website name.

B. Thumbnails for each open site display.

C. The tabs display in the order they were opened.

2 On the taskbar, point to the **Internet Explorer** icon 🅴. What is the result?

A. Thumbnail images for each tab display.

B. All the sites close.

C. A menu displays to close all tabs.

3 On a **New tab**, go to the site **mdc.edu**, and then click the **View favorites** button. Click **Add to favorites**. What is your result?

A. The Favorites Center pane displays on the left side of the screen.

B. The Create Favorites Folder dialog box displays.

C. The Add a Favorite dialog box displays.

4 Click **Cancel**. On the displayed home page for **Miami Dade College**, point to the link for **Academic Programs** to display the 🖑 pointer, and then right-click. From the displayed shortcut menu, which of the following actions are possible?

A. You can open the Academic Programs link in a new tab.

B. You can send the Academic Programs link to your Documents folder.

C. You can create a tab group.

(Project 1D Use Desktop Internet Explorer 11 continues on the next page)

CHAPTER REVIEW

5 Click in a blank area of the screen to close the shortcut menu. Click the **View favorites** button to open the **Favorites** pane. Across the top, which tabs display?

A. Favorites, Tab Groups, Feeds

B. Favorites, Feeds, History

C. Favorites, History, Recent Pages

6 Click the **History tab**, and then click the **arrow**. Which of the following is *not* a viewing arrangement?

A. By Date

B. By Favorites

C. By Most Visited

7 Click in a blank area of the screen to close **Favorites** pane. On the **Command bar**, click the **Safety** button, and then click **Delete browsing history**. According to this information, cookies consist of:

A. Saved information that you have typed into forms.

B. Files stored on your computer by websites to save preferences.

C. Buttons added to the tab row.

8 **Close** the **Delete Browsing History** dialog box. Click the **Tools** button, and then click **Manage add-ons**. At the bottom of the screen, click **Find more toolbars and extensions**. What is your result?

A. A list of add-ons stored on your computer displays.

B. A list of recently used add-ons displays.

C. The Microsoft site for Internet Explorer Gallery displays.

9 **Close** the **Internet Explorer Gallery** site and the **Manage Add-ons** window. Open a **New tab**, and then at the bottom, click **Start InPrivate Browsing**. What is your result?

A. The Delete Browsing History dialog box displays.

B. A new window opens in which you can type a URL in the address box.

C. Both A and B.

10 **Close** the **InPrivate** window and **Close** the New tab. With the **Miami Dade College** site displayed, click the **Print button arrow**, and then click **Print preview**. Click the **Page Setup** button to display the **Page Setup** dialog box. From this dialog box, which of the following can be changed?

A. Left and right margins

B. Headers and Footers

C. Both A and B.

To complete this project: On the taskbar, click the **Word** button, and then type your answers into the correct boxes. **Save** and **Close** your Word document, and submit as directed by your instructor. **Close** ☒ all open windows.

END | You have completed Project 1D

CONTENT-BASED ASSESSMENTS

Mastering Internet Explorer 11	Project 1E Navigate with Internet Explorer 11

In the following Mastering Internet Explorer 11 project, you will open a group of websites on separate tabs. You will capture and save a screenshot that will look similar to Figure 1.51.

PROJECT FILES

For Project 1E, you will need the following file:

New Screenshot

You will save your file as:

Lastname_Firstname_1E_Gov_Tabs

PROJECT RESULTS

FIGURE 1.51

National Institute of Health

(Project 1E Navigate with Internet Explorer 11 continues on the next page)

CONTENT-BASED ASSESSMENTS

1 Display your **Start screen**, and then click the **Internet Explorer** tile. In the **address bar**, click to select the existing text, type **bls.gov** and then press Enter.

2 Open a tab for each of the following sites:

- **defense.gov**
- **state.gov**
- **ed.gov**
- **nih.gov**

3 Display the **tabs bar**, and then create a screenshot that displays the **tabs bar** with each of the five sites displayed. Create a screenshot, copy the screenshot to your **Internet Explorer 11 Chapter 1** folder, and then rename the file as **Lasname_Firstname_1E_Gov_Tabs** Submit this file as directed by your instructor.

4 **Close** all open windows and **Close** Internet Explorer.

END | You have completed Project 1E

CONTENT-BASED ASSESSMENTS

Mastering Internet Explorer 11	Project 1F Using Desktop Internet Explorer

In the following Mastering Internet Explorer 11 project, you will open related sites on separate tabs, and then capture and save a screenshot that will look similar to Figure 1.52.

PROJECT FILES

For Project 1F, you will need the following file:

New Screenshot

You will save your file as:

Lastname_Firstname_1F_Sites

PROJECT RESULTS

FIGURE 1.52

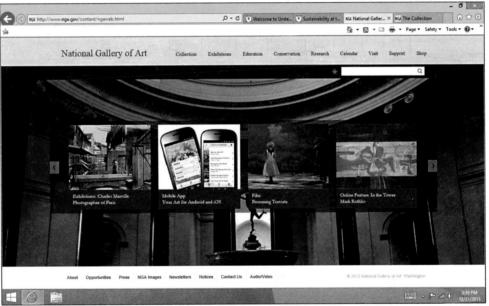

National Gallery of Art

(Project 1F Using Desktop Internet Explorer continues on the next page)

CONTENT-BASED ASSESSMENTS

1 From the taskbar on your desktop, open **Internet Explorer** and be sure only the tab for your home page displays. Click in the **address bar**, type **usbg.gov** and press Enter. Hold down Ctrl, and then in the navigation bar in this site, click **SUSTAINABILITY** so that a new tab is created for the link and the two tabs are color coded.

2 On a **New tab**, go to the site **nga.gov**. Hold down Ctrl, and then in the navigation bar of this site, click **Collection** so that a new tab is created for the link and the two tabs are color coded.

3 Create a screenshot, copy the screenshot to your **Internet Explorer 11 Chapter 1** folder, and then rename it as **Lasname_Firstname_1F_Sites** Submit this file as directed by your instructor.

4 **Close** all open windows and **Close** Internet Explorer.

END | You have completed Project 1F

OUTCOMES-BASED ASSESSMENTS

RUBRIC

The following outcomes-based assessments are *open-ended assessments*. That is, there is no specific correct result; your result will depend on your approach to the information provided. Make *Professional Quality* your goal. Use the following scoring rubric to guide you in *how* to approach the problem, and then to evaluate *how well* your approach solves the problem.

The *criteria*—Software Mastery, Content, Format and Layout, and Process—represent the knowledge and skills you have gained that you can apply to solving the problem. The *levels of performance*—Professional Quality, Approaching Professional Quality, or Needs Quality Improvements—help you and your instructor evaluate your result.

	Your completed project is of Professional Quality if you:	Your completed project is Approaching Professional Quality if you:	Your completed project Needs Quality Improvements if you:
1-Software Mastery	Choose and apply the most appropriate skills, tools, and features and identify efficient methods to solve the problem.	Choose and apply some appropriate skills, tools, and features, but not in the most efficient manner.	Choose inappropriate skills, tools, or features, or are inefficient in solving the problem.
2-Content	Construct a solution that is clear and well organized, contains content that is accurate, appropriate to the audience and purpose, and is complete. Provide a solution that contains no errors in spelling, grammar, or style.	Construct a solution in which some components are unclear, poorly organized, inconsistent, or incomplete. Misjudge the needs of the audience. Have some errors in spelling, grammar, or style, but the errors do not detract from comprehension.	Construct a solution that is unclear, incomplete, or poorly organized; contains some inaccurate or inappropriate content; and contains many errors in spelling, grammar, or style. Do not solve the problem.
3-Format & Layout	Format and arrange all elements to communicate information and ideas, clarify function, illustrate relationships, and indicate relative importance.	Apply appropriate format and layout features to some elements, but not others. Overuse features, causing minor distraction.	Apply format and layout that does not communicate information or ideas clearly. Do not use format and layout features to clarify function, illustrate relationships, or indicate relative importance. Use available features excessively, causing distraction.
4-Process	Use an organized approach that integrates planning, development, self-assessment, revision, and reflection.	Demonstrate an organized approach in some areas, but not others; or, use an insufficient process of organization throughout.	Do not use an organized approach to solve the problem.

OUTCOMES-BASED ASSESSMENTS

Problem Solving Project 1G Help Desk

In this project, you will construct a solution by applying any combination of the skills you practiced from the Objectives in Projects 1A and 1B.

For Project 1G, you will need the following file:

ie01_1G_Help_Desk

You will save your document as:

Lastname_Firstname_1G_Help_Desk

From the student files that accompany this textbook, open the **Chapter_Files** folder, and then in **Chapter_01** folder, locate and open the Word form **ie01_1G_Help_Desk**. Save the document in your chapter folder as **Lastname_Firstname_1G_Help_Desk**

The following email question has arrived at the Help Desk from an employee at the Bell Orchid Hotels' corporate office. In the Word form, construct a response based on your knowledge of Internet Explorer 11. Although an email response is not as formal as a letter, you should still use good grammar, good sentence structure, professional language, and a polite tone. Save your document and submit the response as directed by your instructor.

To: Help Desk

I have asked my research assistant to conduct some Internet research about what hotels around the country are doing in regard to designing innovative restaurants. Is there a way he could organize the sites he wants me to review by geographic location and by type of restaurant?

END | You have completed Project 1G

OUTCOMES-BASED ASSESSMENTS

Problem Solving | Project 1H Help Desk

In this project, you will construct a solution by applying any combination of the skills you practiced from the Objectives in Projects 1A and 1B.

For Project 1H, you will need the following file:

ie01_1H_Help_Desk

You will save your document as:

Lastname_Firstname_1H_Help_Desk

From the student files that accompany this textbook, open the **Chapter_Files** folder, and then in the **Chapter_01** folder, locate and open the Word form **ie01_1H_Help_Desk**. Save the document in your chapter folder as **Lastname_Firstname_1H_Help_Desk**

The following email question has arrived at the Help Desk from an employee at the Bell Orchid Hotels' corporate office. In the Word form, construct a response based on your knowledge of Internet Explorer 11. Although an email response is not as formal as a letter, you should still use good grammar, good sentence structure, professional language, and a polite tone. Save your document and submit the response as directed by your instructor.

To: Help Desk

Guests who use the computers in our hotel Business Centers have inquired about how they can prevent others from seeing the sites they visited and potentially seeing personal information. What instructions could we post at each of these computers to advise guests how to remove any such information from these public computers?

END | You have completed Project 1H

OUTCOMES-BASED ASSESSMENTS

Problem Solving | Project 1I Help Desk

In this project, you will construct a solution by applying any combination of the skills you practiced from the Objectives in Projects 1A and 1B.

For Project 1I, you will need the following file:

ie01_1I_Help_Desk

You will save your document as:

Lastname_Firstname_1I_Help_Desk

From the student files that accompany this textbook, open the **Chapter_Files** folder, and then in the **Chapter_01** folder, locate and open the Word form **ie01_1I_Help_Desk**. Save the document in your chapter folder as **Lastname_Firstname_1I_Help_Desk**

The following email question has arrived at the Help Desk from an employee at the Bell Orchid Hotels' corporate office. In the Word form, construct a response based on your knowledge of Internet Explorer 11. Although an email response is not as formal as a letter, you should still use good grammar, good sentence structure, professional language, and a polite tone. Save your document and submit the response as directed by your instructor.

To: Help Desk

Guests commonly stop by the Front Desk at our hotels and inquire about what the weather will be like in the next few days. Is there a way we could have something on all of the Front Desk computers that would provide the Desk Clerks with constantly updated weather information?

END | You have completed Project 1I

Index

Pearson MyLabs and Mastering

PROVEN RESULTS

For over 10 years, instructors and students have reported better grades through increased engagement and real-time insights into progress.

ENGAGING EXPERIENCES

Pearson MyLab and Mastering programs are designed to reach students in a personal way. Engaging learning and practice opportunities lead to assessments that create a personalized study plan.

A TRUSTED PARTNERSHIP

With millions of students registered annually, Pearson MyLab and Mastering programs are the most effective and reliable learning solutions available today.

For more information, visit: http://www.myitlab.com

ISBN-13: 978-0-13-384763-5

www.pearsonhighered.com

PEARSON

ALWAYS LEARNING